Singing Out

A FOLK NARRATIVE OF
MADDY PRIOR,
JUNE TABOR &
LINDA THOMPSON

SINGING OUT

A FOLK NARRATIVE OF
MADDY PRIOR,
JUNE TABOR &
LINDA THOMPSON

By David Burke

soundcheck books
the stories behind the sounds

First published in Great Britain in 2015 by Soundcheck Books LLP,
88 Northchurch Road, London, N1 3NY.
Copyright © David Burke 2015
ISBN: 978-0-9929480-2-3

A CIP record for this book is available from the British Library
Book design: Benn Linfield (www.bennlinfield.com)
Printed by: Bell & Bain Ltd, Glasgow

For my brilliant boy Dylan,
who's about to write his own exciting narrative.

CONTENTS

♪

ACKNOWLEDGEMENTS

℘

Firstly, my immense gratitude to the three subjects of this book, Maddy, June and Linda, for giving generously of their time to answer questions they must have heard God knows how many times before. Maddy really is as earthy as you've heard, while June, in conversation, is far removed from the austere persona she seems to have unwittingly cultivated through her music. My interviews with Linda were conducted via email – "David, would love to chat, but I can't speak on the phone. Speech pretty non-existent at the moment," she wrote in one of our early exchanges. We can only hope that she recovers sufficiently from the dysphonia that has plagued her since the 1970s, to enhance the world some more with the gift of her voice. Interviews not conducted by me personally are credited in the Notes & Sources section of the book.

Thanks a million also to (in alphabetical order) Ian Anderson, Les Barker, Mike Batt, Eric Bogle, Joe Boyd, Mike Brocken, Louise Cullen, Martin Carthy, Barbara Charone, Sharon Chevin, Ted Cummings, Andy Cutting, Karen Demeusy, Troy Donockley, Mark Emerson, Phil and Sue Godsell at Soundcheck Books, Jake Guralnick, Antony Hegarty, Hannah James, Mac MacLeod, Shaun MacDonald, my very good buddy Sean McGhee at R2, Christy Moore, Simon Nicol, Jenna Ruggiero, Ann Savoy, Denise Sergeant, Ron Sexsmith, Harriet Simms, Martin Simpson, Britta Sweers, David Thomas, Ian Telfer, Teddy Thompson, Rufus Wainwright, Victoria Walker (another beautiful and spirited woman), Huw Warren and Andrew Watts.

Finally, and most importantly, to Shirley, without whom nothing would make any sense. May your heart always be joyful and your song always be sung.

INTRODUCTION

ʃ

It's a tricky course to plot. Three subjects, each worthy of their own tome, each of whom has left an indelible mark on the landscape of British folk music, however much they may have drifted from this landscape over the decades. You could, of course, pluck any three women from the so-called second revival of the 1960s, and follow the trajectory of their respective vocations (artists, particularly those in the folk idiom, don't have careers) from then to now. Shirley and Dolly Collins, Anne Briggs, Sandy Denny, Sonja Kristina, Jacqui McShee, Norma and Lal Waterson, for instance. So why this particular triumvirate? Put simply, because Maddy Prior, June Tabor and Linda Thompson have both endured and evolved. The people's relationship with its heritage may be capricious, but Maddy, June and Linda have remained resolutely committed to it while concurrently contemporising it.

They have stayed true to the ethos of the cultural revolution from which they emerged, an ethos that, essentially, transposes what was into what is, that places the past in the present. They continue to record and, with the exception of Linda (afflicted by spasmodic dysphonia, a cruel condition that subdues her vocal cords), to perform live. They are, in other words, still relevant after all these years. They got their start in the folk clubs that were omnipresent back in the day, singing from the floor, learning the tradition while absorbed in that tradition. An apprenticeship of a kind that defined their subsequent development, where the old songs are made new and the new songs are made old. It doesn't matter that Maddy's beloved Steeleye Span plugged in and wigged out, that June hung with jazzheads, or that Linda spilled the blood of her decomposing marriage to Richard Thompson on the tracks and on stage – their folk roots have always shown through. They have never forgotten the origins from which they came. *Singing Out* returns to those origins, tracking an impressionistic narrative path through biography and analysis, and conversations with Maddy, June and Linda, along with many of their collaborators, in attempting to convey a real sense of the trio as women and a sense of their import as artists.

David Burke 2015

— One —

Banging The Drum For Blighty

♩

There remains some debate about just when it began. The general consensus among those who record such things – anoraks and academics largely (musicians aren't that bothered) – places the advent of the second British folk revival at the outset of the 1950s. When it ended – and if indeed it did – is a whole other, far more protracted, debate altogether. Of course, whether you can actually revive something that is extant is a moot point. Better not to get bogged down in semantics here though, but rather accept that there was a second revival.

Which means there had to be a first. The history books suggest this straddled the late 19th and early 20th centuries, and was spearheaded by collectors intent on preserving indigenous folk and dance. Collectors such as Sabine Baring-Gould, Frank Kidson, Lucy Broadwood, Anne Gilchrist and, perhaps the best known of them all, Francis James Child, an American scholar whose eight-volume *The English And Scottish Popular Ballads* – alias the Child Ballads – was a landmark anthology. And then there was Cecil Sharp, founder of the English Folk Dance Society (which later merged with the Folk Song Society to create the English Folk Dance and Song Society), a somewhat divisive figure among folkies. His popular image is that "of a charming eccentric cycling around Somerset knocking on people's doors, persuading old ladies to sing him their lovely old songs so he could save them from extinction".[1] The alternative view vilifies Sharp as "a controlling manipulator who presented a false idyll of rural England by excluding anything that didn't fit his agenda".[2]

The curative efforts of Child, Sharp and others seemed of little relevance to the Britain that emerged in the aftermath of the Second World War. Safeguarding heritage wasn't high on the agenda of a nation that needed physical rebuilding. And besides, communities "appeared to reject their music even more strongly as unwanted reminders of their class and pre-war lifestyles".[3] Something similar happened in my own native Ireland when the Brits were finally banished – from the south at least – after eight centuries of occupation. For a long time we preferred to forget anything that pitched us back into the past. It was, quite literally, another country. The old songs were redolent of a history that was anathema to a people trying to discover itself anew.

There were certain revisionists who banged the drum for Blighty "in different ways and with different motivations", according to Dr Mike Brocken, senior lecturer in music at Liverpool Hope University. "It ranged from choral societies and Co-op choirs singing traditional songs, to (Benjamin) Britten and Peter Peers recording traditional material, to Rolf Gardiner and his fascist chums wanting musical purity," he says.

But these rather disparate lobbies aside, tradition – especially traditional music – was marginalised on the whole. Dr Britta Sweers, Professor of Cultural Anthropology of Music at the University of Bern, while researching her book, *Electric Folk: The Changing Face Of English Traditional Music*, uncovered an interesting theory for this:

> With regard to the disappearance of traditional music, many traditional communities perceived the First World War as a significant point of change, as many male performers had died during the war. The impact of the war itself was not an issue in the discourses after the Second World War. Rather, we find a stronger socio-cultural discourse. Reports and descriptions indicated that rural and working class traditions were perceived as outdated. Within this context, traditional music was also perceived as an outdated marker of class differences. In some cases, as with Martin Carthy's father, parents also hid their background in traditional music from their children due to their Irish background, which they had experienced as highly problematic in Britain in the 1950s.

♪

Martin Carthy, one of the fountainheads of British, or more pertinently, English folk, was a seminal influence on both Bob Dylan and Paul Simon (who used his arrangement of "Scarborough Fair" for Simon & Garfunkel's 1966 album *Parsley, Sage, Rosemary And Thyme*), and has been omnipresent for more than half a century, whether solo or as a member at various intervals of The Watersons, Steeleye Span, The Albion Country Band and The Imagined Village. He is a fascinating, sagacious interviewee, who, rather than adhering to the call and response that determines the fundamental rule of engagement with enquirers such as myself, embarks on the kind of discursive diversions that are both educative and entertaining and, eventually, make perfect sense. Apropos of which, I give you his labyrinthine theory on the folk culture disconnect between the first and second revivals.

"When I first heard Sam Larner sing, this young fisherman, when I was about 17, I was completely blown away. The thing that knocked me out was how strange the music was. At that time I sort of wanted to sing English folk songs, but I imagined that I automatically had this connection with English music. Also, I had just seen Ravi Shankar for the first time. When I heard Sam Larner I realised that the music he was doing was as exotic – it wasn't as brilliant in that technical sense – but it was as foreign to me. What he was doing was something I just didn't understand. I knew that he meant every word he sang because he kept landing on the root note, he kept landing on doh. I was totally thunderstruck. I remember walking away thinking, 'What the hell have I just heard?' That propelled me into a deeper interest. Then I eventually came to understand that one of the great things about folk music is that it's bloody hard. It's hard stuff. So there is no automatic connection between my Englishness and English folk music. It doesn't exist.

"Another thing that occurred to me about fifteen or twenty years ago, was that whatever was done to the Irish, the Scots and the Welsh was done to the English first – just about everything. Famines and stuff like that. I don't know how many people were killed. The people who were in charge basically didn't give a shit about the people underneath. I'm going back a very long way. There were clearances in England. The Scots talk rightly about the clearances and the effect of them, but there were clearances in England 300 years before. The clearance I was told about, and which I have no reason to dispute, was round about 1496 in what's now Northamptonshire.

"Winston Churchill in the Second World War – he was the man for the job. But in the First World War, the fact that he came bottom in geography at Harrow marked him out. He was the person who, I think, was responsible for Gallipoli. In the Second World War he was the person responsible for the Allied landings in Italy, saying, 'We will strike at the soft underbelly of Europe'. The soft underbelly was a mountainous thing called Italy. The terrain was something else. His knowledge of geography didn't help him to understand that. It's salutary that in the first election after 1945, people rejected him out of hand because they knew about his record. They knew he'd done a great job but it was a case of, 'No thank you, that's enough. We want something else. You've served your purpose'

"English people were as battered as bruised as anybody, and they had it worse. That's one contributory factor. Also, in the First World War, how many millions of people from these shores were killed? The Irish were lucky in that you had the Irish Sea, so your folk music, while not exactly in rude health, was in pretty bloody good nick. The Scots, to a certain extent, had a certain bloody-mindedness and their tradition, again, was in pretty good nick. The fiddle tradition had moved over to Nova Scotia, because of the clearances. So great was the crime committed against the Scots, that the whole thing moved wholesale across the Atlantic, with a considerable loss of life. The Welsh got the crap beaten out of them for speaking Welsh. The British – I'll call them the British – they decided everybody should be standard, so they beat the crap out of the Welsh for speaking Welsh, they beat the crap out of the Scots for speaking Gaelic, and tried to do the same to the Irish.

"They did similar things to England. There's a coat – I think it's in the Dorchester museum – with, I believe it's a penny sewn into the lining. If you were picked up on the road and you had a penny on you, you weren't destitute, so you couldn't be arrested. Otherwise you could be taken into custody. A whole repression was going on. It's a contributory factor. That and events like war, and the cost of it in human life, are the sorts of things that undermine tradition. Why something like Morris dancing became an object of ridicule is beyond me. When I see kids do it, it's amazingly athletic and beautiful to watch. It's a fantastic experience. I used to think – and part of me still does think – that they decided people needed tradition. So they actually replaced the traditions. One of our traditions now is Trooping the Colour. It's got to be visible and there's a million reasons for it happening. I've had discussions with Dick Gaughan over this and he agrees."

Phew!

¶

Commensurate with Britain's post-war rejection of its ancestral mores, was the increasing importation – the jingoists would probably say infiltration – of American culture, particularly pronounced in the realm of music. Rock'n'roll and all that.

This was where Ewan MacColl and A.L. (Bert) Lloyd came in. MacColl, born James Miller, grew up in Lancashire of Scottish descent. His father, an iron moulder, was a militant trade unionist, an ideological path followed by the son, who, as a teenage factory worker, became a member of the Young Communist League and was a regular on the picket line. Influenced by Bertolt Brecht, poet, playwright and avowed Marxist, he started writing songs around the same time as his political awakening. A decade on, MacColl relocated to London, where, after trying his hand as an actor, he turned his attention to traditional music, as both a singer and collector.

Lloyd, meanwhile, was raised in Sussex and London. His father was invalided in the First World War and, when his mother died in 1924, he was despatched, as a young man, to Australia through the British Legion to find employment on farms and sheep stations. Returning to England in the 1930s, Lloyd allied himself with a group of left-wing intellectuals – among them Welsh poet Dylan Thomas – and joined the Communist Party. He combined private studies of folk music with playing the music itself (even winning the EFDSS Folk Music Festival Competition at Cecil Sharp House in 1948), and presented several shows on the subject for the BBC before committing himself to the vocation of folklorist full-time.

Lloyd met MacColl in the early 1950s, and the so-called second folk revival had its pioneers. The two men, each fired by a common cause, embarked on a crusade to create an authentic English music. Their objective was to popularise the English folk music of the 19th century, especially sea shanties, classic ballads and industrial songs, "to convince the younger generation that this music was as vital and good as American popular music".[4] This was initially accomplished through BBC radio broadcasts *Ballads And Blues* and *As I Roved Out*, and releases on Topic Records. MacColl also established one of the first folk clubs in 1953, the no-frills Ballad and Blues Club in the heart of the capital's Soho district.

"Members of the second revival were mainly performing, singing and/or playing instruments. Collecting played a comparably small role," says Dr Britta Sweers.

"Rather, the collected material of the first revival became the reference source for the second revival. Direct contact with performers played a much smaller role. Many performers of the second revival did not grow up with the material they would later adapt as their musical identity.

"We can observe an expansion of repertoire. The first revival was clearly shaped by late Victorian morals, which partly led to a change of phrases etc. in the printed collections. Furthermore, the second revival also included material that might not have been regarded as 'proper' rural-traditional material by the first one, such as sea shanties and industrial folk music."

Topic's role in the revival can't be understated. Or, as June Tabor put it to me, "Where would we be without Topic?"

Established in 1939 as an offshoot of the British Marxist Party's educational wing, the Communist-led Workers' Music Association,

Topic originally sold left wing political music by mail order. The war then disrupted production. When it resumed near the end of the 1940s, there was a move towards filling the void in the traditional market. MacColl and Lloyd were heavily involved through the 1950s and 1960s, issuing albums such as *Street Songs And Fiddle Tunes Of Ireland* by Margaret Barry and Michael Gorman, *The Iron Muse* and *The Bird In The Bush*.

Dr Sweers points out Topic's importance "It was the central recording infrastructure for the performers of the second revival. This was significant at a time when major recording companies like HMV or Decca would not have invested in this direction. At the same time, Topic thus became a central recorded source of revival, and also traditional singers. It hereby also had a strong impact on the emerging singing styles."

❡

Yet for all of Lloyd and MacColl's campaigning zeal, the nascent revival failed to gain any real momentum. It was too small scale and possibly too elitist in attracting (if not targeting) the middle class demographic. That was about to change. And such change would be wrought by the emergence of a fad, an ephemeral scene that was, with delicious irony, rooted not in England's green and pleasant land, but across the Atlantic in the United States. It was there that skiffle – a hotchpotch of work songs, spirituals, blues and old English, Scottish and Irish airs brought over by immigrants – had developed in the 1930s. Dismissed as poor man's jazz, the style embraced every conceivable sound device, from the conventional (the guitar) to the creative (washboards, bottles, bowls and the kazoo, which was a comb wrapped in wax paper). Skiffle made its British bow in the 1940s, but didn't really take off until 1956 when Lonnie Donegan hit pay dirt with his Top 10 version of Leadbelly's "Rock Island Line".

The impact on the folk revival was two-fold. Firstly, skiffle democratised the playing of music, which, before then, had been a mainly professional pursuit. Suddenly anyone could pick up an instrument and form a band. John Lennon and Paul McCartney did, so too Hank Marvin, John Renbourn and Rick Kemp. And secondly, it provided an introduction to the folk canon.

As Mike Brocken explains, "It was a great access point, and some of the musical materials were, genre-wise, related to British folk songs. In fact, some skiffle groups played songs such as 'The Derby Ram'."

Dr Sweers adds, "Skiffle provided a first practical musical experience for many future revival musicians. When the skiffle boom faded out around 1958, many performers were looking for new spaces and material to play, and thus partly went into folk clubs. Skiffle thus provided a broad basis of active performers without whom the revival would have probably otherwise just been a very small movement of a few insiders."

As the skiffle clubs that had sprung up in towns and cities transformed into the folk clubs, "young enthusiasts like Martin Carthy, Norma Waterson, Shirley Collins and Bob Davenport began to sing songs from their own heritage".[5]

Waterson recalled how they were "absolutely in thrall to the music – the music is dark, the music is fascinating".[6]

Carthy, a passionate advocate of English tradition – his tradition – has always espoused a progressive rather than puritanical philosophy when it comes to the songs. In a 1988 interview with *The Guardian* newspaper, he railed against what he saw then as England's contempt for its own music. He might as well have been talking about England before the second revival:

> This is not the music of an uptight people, but people who remember a time when you didn't have to pay a licence to make music in a pub. The English don't have any self-regard, they assume their self-respect comes from conquering others. English tradition is now sold very hard as Buckingham Palace, the Tower of London and the rest. I consider that an outrage. Those institutions have nothing to do with the identity of an English people or of a society that now includes all manner of races

In the past, the English tried to impose a system wherever they went. They destroyed the nation's culture and one of the by-products of their systemisation was that they destroyed their own folk culture. They destroyed it by uprooting communities during the Industrial Revolution. The Church cleared up the music, telling the people it was awful, and when the church bands proved too refractory, they booted them out and replaced them with the organ so that they couldn't work. The dances died but the songs take a lot longer to die.[7]

Carthy, just like Maddy Prior, June Tabor and Linda Thompson, came out of the folk club environment that burgeoned in the 1960s. By the middle of that decade there were hundreds in London, some 72 on Merseyside alone, and others in cities like Birmingham, Newcastle, Sheffield, Glasgow and Edinburgh. They were mostly housed above pubs in smoke-filled, bare rooms with few stages and no sound systems at all.

Eric Bogle, the Scottish songwriter who went on to pen "The Band Played Waltzing Matilda" and "No Man's Land" (also known as "The Green Fields Of France"), helped to run the club in his hometown of Peebles. He was drawn to the scene through "a growing involvement in politics and a dawning realisation of the injustices of life in general, issues which folk music often addressed and other forms of music mostly did not". Bogle eventually left Peebles and Scotland for Canberra, Australia, and he proffers an interesting observation of the differences between the folk environments in both countries.

"Folk clubs in Scotland had a wider audience demographic," says Bogle. "A lot of working class people were involved. In Canberra, it was mostly middle class people – students, public servants and the like – singing about the dignity of sweated labour, the coming revolution, peace, love and all that stuff. And also, there were far fewer Aran sweaters in the folk scene in Canberra!"

For Richard Thompson, the folk clubs were "just another place where you'd hear music, you'd even perform sometimes".[8] Yet it was here where the real work of the revival took place, where the living tradition found the air it needed to breathe. Christy Moore made the short journey across the Irish Sea in the mid-1960s because he couldn't make any headway back home.

"There was an emerging scene in Dublin, but I could not fit in. I always felt on the outside," says Moore. "My first experience of an English folk club was in London in 1966 – it might have been called the Scotch House. The guest was Anne Briggs. At the time I was struggling to survive, playing in pubs where songs were not greatly valued. Hearing Anne Brigs sing to a silent and enthralled room was a revelation.

"I moved to Manchester and began to hear a lot of English and Scottish singers. It was such a diverse scene, yet it seemed to me to meld into one. I heard The Watersons, Carthy and (Dave) Swarbrick, MacColl and (Peggy) Seeger, Pentangle, The Young Tradition and The Ian Campbell Group – these were among the bigger names on the circuit. I also knew Martyn Wyndham-Read, Mike Harding, Ralph McTell, Hamish Imlach, Alex Campbell, to name very few of those whom I encountered. Every area had its own coterie of very fine artists. In Manchester, Harry Bradshaw, The Pennine Folk, The Beggarmen; in Leeds, Bob and Carol Pegg, Allen 'Spud' Taylor, Jon Rennard. For me it was a feast of songs and music everywhere I landed.

"Meeting Mike Harding in 1966 was a revelation for me. He encouraged me and gave me my first gig. I used to go to the Singers' Club every Monday in the Manchester Sports Guild, which back then was the mecca of folk in the north west of England. I found that I was accepted as a singer and did not encounter any resistance to my emerging repertoire.

"I was never seeking any particular community – I simply wanted to be a singer. I had worked at many different jobs in my young life, but failed at every one. The English and Scottish folk clubs gave me the opportunities and encouragement I needed to begin making my way. There was no such thing as a typical club. Some were trad., others contemporary, some favoured comedy acts, others sea shanties. I tried to play them all."

♪

Like any living thing, the folk clubs adapted to the prevailing milieu. The times they certainly were a-changing, and so too was folk music. MacColl's vision was no longer shared by the younger emerging folkies, who were intent on reconfiguring the revival, determined to remould it in their own contemporary image. There was revolution in the ranks, a rejection of the hard line policies enforced at the Singers' Club on London's Old Brompton Road (formerly the Ballad and Blues Club), where MacColl "gave the world the image of the British folkie as a bearded reactionary in an Aran sweater, singing with finger in ear... he seems to have spent an awful lot of time bossing everyone else around, with contention predictably resulting".[9] He also ran the Critics' Club out of the Beckenham flat MacColl shared with Peggy Seeger, half-sister of American folk hero Pete Seeger. This was a loosely organised company of singers who trained in folk singing and theatre techniques.

Maddy Prior thought the Singers' Club "very cliqueish... Ewan had a wonderful sense of the romantic, but desperately wanted to be taken seriously. It was such a shame, because all his good songs were the romantic ones, not the political ones which are fucking awful."[10]

Christy Moore described his appearance at the Singers' Club in 1968 as a turning point, and appreciated "MacColl for recognising my nervousness and giving a few words of comfort and a dram of whiskey to settle me down".[11]

Expounding on that watershed moment for this book, Moore says, "A year before I played the Singers' Club I got to know Ralph McTell. He introduced me to his brother, Bruce May, who was then Ralph's manager. Bruce came to my gig at the Troubadour in London. Afterwards he had some harsh words for me, but words I needed to hear. He told me to stop trying to be a 'stage Paddy', that if I took my work more seriously, others might do likewise. To this day I am grateful for that advice. I began to do just what he suggested and eighteen months later played at gig at the Singers' Club in the Union Tavern in London. I shared a stage with Ewan MacColl and Peggy Seeger. I would consider this to have been one of the most prestigious gigs of my life. I cannot explain why, it's just the way I feel. However, I will always be a bit of a 'stage Paddy', and why not? I'm a bog man – deep down it's where I come from."

From the off, Moore was beguiled by MacColl's songs, even before he'd heard the name. "He had quite a reputation around the circuits, not all of it favourable. When I got a gig at MacColl and Seeger's club in 1969, none of the things I had heard about them were apparent to me that night nor subsequently. His influence is enormous, even upon people who have never heard his name. His songs remain in my repertoire 50 years on. His songs are known all over Ireland, yet most people do not know his name. That says a lot about Ewan MacColl."

Martin Carthy reckons MacColl's quixotic attitude was, in fact, a courageous one. "He stuck his head above the parapet. He made himself a target. He wanted people to sing their own songs and that's an interesting thing to do to people who have lost it. He said, 'Go and find it'. There are some interesting and fascinating things to be found, and some things that will consume you because they are so exciting. It's thrilling what you can actually collect – and it's never ending. I get asked at my age, 'Why don't you retire?' Because there's too much to do! Too much to find out. People who are totally unschooled make the most exciting decisions about what they're going to do when they sing. It's not orthodox, by God it's not, but it's sophisticated."

The museum-like culture engendered by MacColl and his acolytes was "all a bit too rigid" for Maddy Prior. "I'm not that sort of person, really. It sort of appealed to me intellectually, but not as a performer. I remember hearing all this stuff about how you must let the song come through you, how it's not about you. But then I went to Loughborough Festival and saw Davie Stewart and Jimmy MacBeath, and they sold their songs like crazy. They weren't standing there letting the song come through them! I thought, 'This is a load of bollocks'.

"The song is the most important thing. The material is what makes a musician. If you are good enough you animate the song. You can make a song pretty deadly if you're not good. You can be the best performer in the world, but if you've not got the material then it becomes a technical thing."

Tim Hart, Prior's former duet partner, dismissed the folk clubs as "too introspective and too amateur. I didn't think they did the music any favours at all. It was a very eclectic little thing – folk music went on in upstairs rooms in pubs, and you had to sit very quietly through it. If you weren't the right sort of person, if you didn't fit in, you couldn't listen to folk music – it was totally bloody silly."[12]

Anne Briggs, a reluctant star of the folk revival whose unaccompanied 1964 EP, *The Hazards Of Love*, proved a touchstone for Maddy and for June Tabor, believed the only thread that ran through the tradition was "a gut feeling... the direct line that some singers had through singing those songs through human emotion".[13]

What Prior and Briggs were talking about was evolving the songs – not merely channelling but charging the narratives with their own experiences and personalities, making them resonate in their own time. If MacColl and his ilk were not impressed by such exposition, they were positively incensed by what emanated next from the traditional template – electric folk. Pentangle, with their extended instrumental passages, unorthodox rhythms and open tunings, were close enough for jazz. The Incredible String Band's experimental approach presaged the world music boom of the 1990s, whilst Fairport Convention and Steeleye Span emphasised bass and drums for a tougher sonic edge.

Yet Dr Sweers believes that MacColl's dogmatic stance unwittingly helped to create electric folk. "It seems that his dogmatism was actually driving a lot of performers out of the clubs in search of alternative spaces which they found in the collaboration with rock and jazz musicians. On the other hand, this likewise stimulated a musical counter-movement that contributed to the emergence of electric folk."

Professor Mike Brock insists electric folk was a wholly separate entity from the folk revival, which "by and large it came from rock bands interested in folk, not the other way round".

Whatever its provenance, it provoked an extreme response from some within the traditional folk fraternity. "A lot of people didn't like it, especially when we started using amplifiers. I started getting death threats," said Danny Thompson, Pentangle's double bassist. At least Bob Dylan only had to contend with booing and accusations of betrayal.

— Two —

Songs About People

♪

Maddy Prior was made in Blackpool. It was in the Lancashire seaside town where she spent her formative years and developed attitudes that were "quite puritan, in a funny way".

Her dad was Allan Prior, a native Geordie, scriptwriter and novelist who worked on some 78 episodes of the BBC police drama, *Z-Cars*, and contributed to its spin-off, *Softly, Softly*. During a prolific career on the small screen, he also contributed to *Blake's Seven*, *Dr Finlay's Casebook*, *The Onedin Line*, *The Sweeney* and *Juliet Bravo*, while his fiction won him the Crime Writers' Association Award on two occasions.

"The creative life, the artistic world, was always there and always available, and a happy choice in some senses for my parents, which made it easier for me," Maddy said of her upbringing.

"They supported me in what I wanted to do. I think it was also the fact that I was a girl and therefore was expected to marry in those days, so it wasn't essential that I, for instance, had a proper job. Perhaps if I had been a boy it might have been different."[14]

There was a downside to her father being in his chosen profession. "I didn't start writing songs until I was nearly 30. I think my reluctance was partly due to my father being a writer, and I steered away from it."[15]

Expounding on the subject for *Singing Out*, she says: "My father was a very crafted and skilled writer – very disciplined. The idea, even now, of being that disciplined is beyond me. He wrote every day. It was like a drug. He had his own system for it. So he didn't start writing until four in the afternoon and he'd finish at eight.

15

"When I started writing, you realise a song is a whole different thing from a novel, or a script for television. There's much more discipline involved in that, and I'm not a disciplined writer. I write when it comes or when there's a requirement for it. To write a good song is an amazing thing. It may not be true of all writing, but you've got to be inspired – you've got to have an idea. For instance, with journalism there's a story to be got and you have to find what that story is, then it's a case of writing it. For me, the idea is almost 80% of the song, because what the song is saying is what's important. Then if you can make it work with a tune, that's the genius.

"I think the very first song I wrote – and it didn't have any impact – was a song called 'Magpie', which I sang more recently on an album (*Seven For Old England*). I wrote it when I was about 18. I was working with Tim Hart. It didn't have any impact on him; I thought it wasn't worth it. I sort of quite liked it but I didn't have the confidence to sing it. It's a bit like if you haven't written before, there's not the support for it. Now there is – things have changed. Everybody supports children who write.

"Sandy Denny had the same thing. I don't think anybody was keen for her to do 'Who Knows Where The Time Goes?' Gradually they realised she wrote quite nice songs! And, of course, then there was a little case of, 'Oh, it's only a girl'. Not entirely. And I wouldn't say that was the motivating thing. But music was much more of a man's thing when I was young. Girls were singers. It wasn't that big a deal, and I'm sure in a sense they didn't think of it that way, but it was the way it was presented to us. It was historical.

"I did write a song with my dad once, a thing called 'Never Been Kissed'. He did a book about the music halls. I wrote this tune and a verse. I couldn't think of any other verses. So he said, 'Alright, I'll see if I can put something together. What have you got?' So I gave him the tune and he fiddled and farted about with it one day. And, obviously, it's a bit like a performance in that he mentally prepared. Then he sat down and he was like a terrier with this thing. That was a lesson. When he did it, he wouldn't let go until it was finished. I thought, 'Oh, right – this is how you do it'. So that went in a bit. Once you start with a song, you need to do it then. It's no use wandering off. You need to try and get it as tight as you can. It's very particular. He encouraged me to write, but I don't remember him giving me pointers. I don't think he thought that was going to be my direction, particularly."

It was her father, however, who identified Maddy as a singer early on, and sent her to have lessons. "I joined Miss Whiteside's Co-op Choir," she recalls. "I didn't really learn much in the way of technique. In fact, I've never learned much in the way of technique, for some reason!"

Maddy would go to the local cinema on Saturdays and take part in singing competitions before the screenings. "I'd sing 'The Tennessee Wig Walk'. I could never understand why until I saw a thing about schoolyards, and apparently in Lancashire that was a song that was sung in the schoolyard. So I'd obviously learned it there. I did it with all the actions and I used to win. If they'd have booed me at that point, that would have been the end of that career, because that's how it works."

The family decamped to St Albans, Hertfordshire, when Maddy was a teenager. The austerity years that immediately followed the Second World War had been supplanted by greater prosperity throughout the 1950s, and the decade proclaimed as the swinging sixties saw an imperceptible shift in the generational axis of power, as younger Britons began to be both seen and heard, particularly in the social environment of the time. Maddy danced to jazz and rock'n'roll – "My idea of a good night out was to dance for four hours. I loved dancing and I was good at it" – and, at 13, was a regular at the folk clubs around the city.

"The folk club was incredibly hip. It was very cool. That was where everybody went," she remembers.

Mac MacLeod first met Maddy when she was a pupil at the girls' grammar school in St Albans. They were, he says, "attracted to each other musically, with our shared interest in folk music. We lived quite close to each other, and so we started working things out round my place – or should I say, my grandmother's place – with a view to performing locally. For me, the interest in music had started with the DIY of skiffle, and then naturally progressed to folk and blues, of which there were now many new clubs and venues, along with a wealth of developing talent."

MacLeod would go on to form power trio Hurdy Gurdy, and later Soft Cloud, Loud Earth. But back in St Albans in the mid-1960s, he was one half of Mac & Maddy.

"Going to the Peahen folk club as part of the audience, Maddy and I met up with another couple, Brian and Lesley, who were more into the traditional side of folk, but wanted to give it a try with the four of us going out as a harmony group, with me on guitar. We had our first gig at the Robin Hood in Potters Bar, and although we did plenty of rehearsing and the standard was improving as we played more places, we gradually drifted apart, with Maddy and I gravitating more towards the American influences. The two of us then started going further afield as a duo, playing material mainly derived from the American folk songbook, or the magazine, *Sing Out*, which was always a good source of obscure favourites."

Among their contemporaries was one Donovan Leitch, alias Donovan, who lived in nearby Berkhamstead. It was Don, as Maddy still affectionately calls him, who turned her on to Bob Dylan.

"It was a rainy Saturday afternoon and we had nothing else to do. About four of us went to the record shop and were looking through the records when Don said, 'Oh, this guy is really good'. So we went into the booth and put the record on. This voice came on and we all laughed! We went, 'Don, what are you on about? This is a load of old bollocks!' We weren't going anywhere because it was raining outside, so we sat there and played it again. Then we heard 'Desolation Row' and we all went, 'Oh, this is a bit good'. He meant it. That was what we got."

Donovan morphed into something of a Dylan clone and much ado was made in the music press about the rivalry between the two. In 2001, he admitted that Dylan was, for him, "a spearhead into protest", adding, "We all had a go at his style. I sounded like him for five minutes – others made a career out of his sound. Like troubadours, Bob and I can write about any facet of the human condition. To be compared was natural, but I am not a copyist."[16]

Nor indeed was he ever a credible rival to Bob – and, let's be candid, anyone who suggests otherwise is, at best, fanciful.

Mac & Maddy took a temporary sabbatical in April 1965, when Donovan asked MacLeod to join him on his first British tour, beginning with the *NME* Poll Winners' Concert at Wembley's Empire Pool, and continuing at venues up and down the country as part of a bill including Wayne Fontana And The Mindbenders and Unit Four Plus Two. When MacLeod hooked up again with Maddy, they concentrated their attention on the London scene, playing at places like Les Cousins and The Scots House.

"We also did some recording at this time," Mac says. "I often wonder what happened to the tapes. In fact, there aren't even any pictures of the two of us performing. The only material evidence I have to show that we actually existed is a business card.

"Towards the end of 1966, things were going well for Maddy and myself, and opportunities were opening up, especially with the help of her father. Then I had an offer come through from Harry Brook, one of my old mates. He'd married a Swedish girl and was living in Stockholm, and having made good contacts in the music business, he wanted me to join him out there. His arrangement of all the details, including somewhere to stay, guaranteed gigs and a record deal, made it a very tempting proposition. I had been moving away from folk roots and more towards blues, and it seemed like a good idea at the time, so I decided to go. On reflection, it was a really dumb thing to do, especially after all the effort that Maddy and I had put into making our duo work."

No matter about MacLeod's hindsight self-recrimination, his decision to pursue a different musical direction certainly didn't appear to bother Maddy back then. During a trip with a friend round the south west of England in a van that used more oil than petrol, she had made up her mind that she was going to pursue the folk thing.

"We fetched up in Newquay and we'd run out of money, she recalls. "So we decided to get a job in a Wimpy bar. I did a week there for ten quid, sleeping in the van all the while. But I did a gig on my own, with a banjo, at the same time for eight quid. And I thought that was a better option than the Wimpy bar. I picked up banjo because there was a lot of American music around the folk clubs at that time. There were some people doing the English thing. Brian Pearson, who was in the Critics' Club, was one of the leading lights in the folk club. But we thought he was odd because he sang in this kind of strange voice. We didn't quite understand."

She played the folk clubs, doing floor spots – often three songs – before the main act went on. "It could be awful, of course. That was one of the problems with the folk club. Sometimes it wasn't very good. But gradually most of us improved. I started out with a lot of Peter, Paul & Mary, Joan Baez, Carolyn Hester... Joan Baez was interesting, of course, because she was singing English songs at the time. I used to do a lot of her stuff. 'Copper Kettle', I sang that with Mac.

"One of the attractions of the folk club was that it was uncritical. I liked that. When I teach now I say, 'Just get the critical thing out of your head and don't think that way if you want to go forward and do things'. I think it was a very good ground for people to learn a whole new way of doing things. And out of it we got some very good performers – a lot of comedians came out of it. They had time to learn. They weren't immediately rejected because they hadn't got it right. We did develop a way of doing it, because we sort of had a common idea. But then you had Nic Jones, who didn't do it the way everyone else did. We all were kind of doing something slightly different."

Maddy cut her teeth on the live circuit not just as a performer, but as a roadie. She drove American bluesman Blind Gary Davis around England in 1966.

"That was interesting," she recalls. "He was eccentric. I learned a bit about what it was like to be blind – how you fill time in a different way. You can't go and do things like you would if you were left to your own devices. His attitudes to things were amazing. He was a character and he liked to drink – and I was told not to let him drink! Well, of course, I couldn't stop him. He used to do this thing of talking to his whiskey. Everyone used to fall over laughing. I got shouted at a lot for being a spoilsport. Then afterwards he'd say, 'Miss Maddy, I done drunk too much'. And his great accolade about me at the end of the tour was, 'Miss Maddy, you make a great nurse!'

"Then I took on roadying a couple called Sandy and Jeanie Darlington. They were American and they sang Appalachian music, which I'd never heard before. So they introduced me to sacred heart music in 1966. And they also said to me, 'For goodness sake, stop singing American songs, you're crap at it!' I was kind of offended, really. But I liked what they did and I wanted to impress them. They had catalogues of tapes of English material, and they said, 'You should learn this'. I thought, 'Oh, blimey!'"

Maddy was a modernist. She didn't have much truck with history. It was all so last century. Punk may have declared 1976 the year zero, but that whole palimpsestic concept of beginning again had already been forged in the 1960s. For Maddy, this presented a paradoxical dilemma. She was plugged into the *zeitgeist* – or, as Mac MacLeod put it, hung with the bohemian set and, "with her beloved Vespa and deerstalker crash hat, also leaned towards the mod camp" – but increasingly found herself part of a movement that was in the business of renewal.

"I'd learned folk music at school, and you didn't want things you'd learned at school – well, I didn't," she remembers. "It was the sixties. Anything authoritarian was not attractive at all. School was an interesting time for me. I worked my way through it, but I didn't really engage with it very much. I sort of did alright at it. I didn't want to be at the top and I didn't want to be at the bottom, so I'd hang around in the middle somewhere.

"My father was a writer and quite radical in his views, which changed enormously through my life. He started off almost Communist – or certainly gave me the impression he was Communist – and by the end was much more right wing. We always had rows about it. He pooh-poohed a lot of the education stuff. I didn't think history was valuable. I didn't think early literature was valuable. It had to be modern.

21

"I wanted to do American Studies at Manchester, but I never got in. It wasn't until I started travelling and these guys, Sandy and Jeanie, said to me, 'Learn these tapes'... So I took these tapes away and wearily listened to them, to what I considered these old voices. But I stuck at it. That's what happens with music. You have to put the time in. For most of us, it happens unconsciously when we're young. But if you want to change and learn about another sort of music, you've got to listen to it and learn what its structures are, what its achievements are and what's valuable to it. You don't get that innocently. You've got to work at it. I just sat with this stuff, and eventually I began to think, 'That one's not bad. I kind of like that one'. And gradually I learned to appreciate it."

Then along came Tim Hart.

§

Maddy and Tim were "the English folk scene's answer to America's Sonny and Cher"[17] – a couple onstage and off. Born in Lincoln, Hart, like Maddy, grew up in St Albans. He worked variously (and briefly in all cases) as a bookbinder, blacksmith, cost clerk, civil servant and hospital washer-up, while flirting with pop as a member of The Rattfinks and other styles before finding his niche at the Peahen, where he met Maddy, who remembers: "We came from similar backgrounds in a way. Sort of middle-class but slightly off the wall, because his father was a vicar and mine was a writer, so we didn't fit in anywhere else particularly. He was a great character, was Tim. He became very interested in folk music. He could see the vision in it. He was a very good poet and writer, good with ideas. He was the one who sort of organised it all, got it all going. I just followed along feeling a little bit insecure, really.

"Funnily enough, I was in a group for a short time with Derek Brimstone from Hemel [Hempstead]. I used to go to the Hemel club. There were three of us – me, Derek and another guy – and we were going to do twenty minutes. I said to Derek one day, 'Of course, I was very shy when I was young'. He said, 'Shy?! Shy? The only reason I talk on stage is because of you! At 15 you told us, "Right, you're going to do the talking".' So maybe I don't see myself broadly as other people do."

As Tim Hart & Maddy Prior, the duo recorded a brace of critically lauded albums for Tepee Records, *Folk Songs Of Olde England Vols 1* and *2*, featuring many compositions they had learned at Cecil Sharp House. She told J.P. Bean, "It definitely moved us up the ladder in the sort of pecking order. It established us because not too many people had albums out at the time."[18]

It was around this time that Maddy also "started to read and become interested in history as well. I started to see the songs as being about people. There were stories that I liked. I started to see beyond the structures and the clothes and the transport system, and see the songs for what they were about."

Hart, who died from lung cancer aged only 61 on Christmas Eve 2009, was an influential figure in this respect. Arguably, he personified the resolution of Maddy's paradoxical dilemma, bringing together old and new in a coalition of sound and style.

Maddy again: "He was a very anarchic kind of person. The sort of clothes he wore, the dandified approach to performing, was so against everything in the folk world, which delighted him. He was not hidebound by what people thought about things. He was slightly eccentric – kind of unputdownable."[19]

Alongside Maddy in the early incarnation of Steeleye Span, he was determined "to bring traditional songs to a global audience and to show that Steeleye Span could share the stage with the biggest rock acts in the world".[20]

But that was still in the future. In 1966, he and Maddy were a big deal, schlepping around England in a Morris Traveller, playing for enthusiastic audiences in the folk clubs.

— Three —

The Art Of Singing

ʃ

Anne Briggs and Belle Stewart were the stimuli, the ones who really convinced June Tabor to think she could become a singer. The way they sang was the way she wanted to sing. Unaccompanied. A difficult art to master, the vocal equivalent of a tightrope walk, a delicate balance between technique and truth.

It was Ewan MacColl who gave Stewart and her family – Highland Scottish travellers – a start at the Singers' Club in 1954. Ostracised by society, The Stewarts Of Blair, as they were known, enjoyed the adulation of folk club audiences not just in Britain, but throughout Europe and in the United States. Belle became the most renowned of them all, a repository of ballads and stories, the self-proclaimed Queen Among The Heather, much sought after by collectors, musicologists and musicians. According to Paul Marsh, she "did an enormous amount to attract young people back to the roots of their own culture", and as a singer "performed with a natural grace and ease that concealed great artistry, always singing from the heart".[21]

Briggs was someone who, in her pomp as the doyenne of folk revival, turned her back on it for motherhood and conservationist, horticultural and natural history pursuits. Her negligible discography of one EP, 1964's *The Hazards Of Love*, and two albums, *Anne Briggs* and *The Time Has Come*, both issued in 1971, belie the extensive breadth of her influence. Christy Moore cited her as "the most influential person for me on the British folk scene",[22] while for Lal and Norma Waterston she was "without doubt the biggest influence on her generation of singers".[23] Perhaps Ken Hunt offered the most

24

profound appraisal of Briggs' gift when he wrote, "Mystique and nostalgia have tinged people's appreciation of her, but what really seduces the ears is the honesty, intensity and quality of what she sings on her old recordings."[24]

Briggs' use of ornamentation in her performance of a song was something June hadn't previously encountered until she bought a copy of *The Hazards Of Love.*

"My sister took me to a record shop in London," explains June. "She'd bought me a little record player and she wanted to buy me a record. So I poked around in the folk section and I found that. I thought it looked interesting. I took it home and, thought, 'Wow, this is a way of singing – this is a way of just using the voice, not needing any backing'. So I listened to that *ad nauseam*, then I listened back, deconstructed it in my head and slowed it right down in my head, then tried to do it very slowly, note by note. It drove my mother mad! I sat in the bathroom for about a month. Good echo, you see. You can hear what you're doing. A bit cold though!

"Then I got *The Stewarts Of Blair* Topic album. This was a completely different style of unaccompanied singing, the travellers' way, the swoops and long held notes, quite a nasal way of singing. I was really captivated by that as well, so I taught myself how to do that too, just by copying the recording. Then the two styles got very gradually mixed in to the way I sang. That's really how I started to develop any sort of style, by listening to and copying two wonderful singers and working out when to do it and when not to do it. In the end, you do it all the time and then gradually you learn that that's less effective than only doing it occasionally."

June came out of Warwickshire, once part of the ancient Anglo-Saxon kingdom of Mercia. The heart of England. In the Tabor household, the only access to music was through the radio. For a while, in her teens, she wanted to be Françoise Hardy, French chanteuse and actress.

"We got a television about 1958-ish," June recollects. "A couple of years after that there were two programmes on the kind of God spot on a Sunday afternoon on television, which had a degree of folk music content. One was called *Hallelujah!* presented by Sydney Carter, and the other was called *Hullabaloo!*, and I think that was on ITV. That was the first time I ever saw Martin Carthy, accompanying a singer called Nadia Cattouse. Something about the music just appealed to me. That was my first exposure to any kind of folk music.

"As a child I loved to sing, anything. Mostly copying things I heard on the radio. I never did have any musical training, ever. I think I probably sang from very soon after I could speak, just by copying things. My mum and dad would sing snatches of popular songs around the house. They had no musical education or training. It was just one of those things you did. The radio gave me an introduction to all sorts of music – a lot of standards and to a degree the pop music of the day, Cliff Richard and that kind of thing."

Appropriately, it was at the Heart of England folk club, above the Fox and Vivian pub in Leamington Spa, where June first sang in public, egged on by a friend. "I didn't really know what a folk club was. My friend said, 'Come on, let's go – you like singing'. So she took me. We weren't old enough to be in a pub. She'd been to a folk club before, so she knew how things worked. Her name was Frances Shelby, so you can blame Frances Shelby for everything that happened afterwards!

"She went up to the person running the night and said, 'My friend sings – will you put her on?' I said, 'Frances, I don't know any folk songs'. And as I'd annoyed people at children's parties for years by standing up and singing songs, I stood up in a folk club when they asked me and sang, 'Michael, Row The Boat Ashore' and 'Kumbuya' – that's all I knew. It literally was a floor spot – you just stood up where you were and sang."

June was enamoured of the scene, the community aspect of it and, of course, the music – a music "that spoke to me in a very particular and strong way". She became a regular at the Heart of England and frequented other clubs in the area too, including Campbells' in Birmingham. Her repertoire expanded – "Michael Row The Boat Ashore" and "Kumbaya" were augmented by Bob Dylan's "Masters Of War" and "The Gates Of Eden".

"I liked the social importance of a folk club," June says. "It was a way of associating with other people with something in common, without it being too confrontational. You could make friends in a general way. We used to meet in a coffee bar before going to the folk club. Then somebody said one night, 'Why are we meeting here? Why don't we just go straight to the pub?' So we did! We used to go out on a Saturday night and go to pubs and sing, or go to the folk club. For someone like me who was an only child of older parents, who had friends at school but not at home, it was a very good way of establishing some kind of social network.

"It's not like going to a disco and having to dance with someone. I think that can be confrontational if you're shy and extremely socially inexperienced. The friends I had came from different social and working backgrounds, but the thing we had in common was the music."

June learned the rudiments of "the art of singing". How not to make mistakes. It was an education that demanded some courage, offering herself up to a roomful of strangers, aesthetically, emotionally and yes, even physically, in the sense that her very flesh and blood was, for however many minutes, the convergence of attention. There was no music to distract from that attention, no adjunct to the naked voice.

"The reason I sang unaccompanied was because I couldn't play an instrument," confides June. "And I never have learned to play an instrument because I'm too bloody lazy! I mean, I have tried. When I was at university I had a go at playing the whistle and the concertina, but I wasn't very good at it. Then eventually I met people who were extremely good at it, and then – and only then – did I start singing with accompaniment.

"But it was a complete revelation to me when I particularly discovered Anne Briggs and Belle Stewart through recordings, that there was some art of unaccompanied singing. That it wasn't just standing up and singing without any instruments. That there was a whole way, to begin with, from song selection right through. This is all something you learn very slowly, by making mistakes and trying to sing songs that don't want to be sung. There are songs that can and should be sung unaccompanied, and the voice is an instrument. To a degree, ornamentation is part of the way of creating an accompaniment with the voice, which is what Anne Briggs was doing. But equally, the song itself is the means of communication without any sort of disguise. And there are songs that can be sung with one voice.

"The majority of modern created songs were written with an accompanying instrument as part of the process of creation. So somebody is writing a song and they're using a guitar, and the guitar forms part of the shape of the tune. If you consider a song to be a circle, most modern songs need the accompaniment to complete the circle, which is why, unless it was written without any accompaniment in the first place – something like Dave Goulder's 'The Easter Tree', for example, which was not written with any accompaniment – then you find when you try and sing it without any accompaniment, something is missing. Whereas traditional songs, by and large – not all of them, most of them – were often sung without any accompaniment. There might be choral songs, but that's a whole different area altogether.

"I only managed to branch out into discovering modern songs once I started working with an accompanist, Martin Simpson. It didn't happen until Maddy Prior and I made the *Silly Sisters* album. I did all sorts of other things. I sang at two bands in university, so I was doing it then but in a completely different way and with different material. I wasn't trying to do my music.

"The whole performing in public, as opposed to just standing up and doing a floor spot, happened in a very gradual way, largely by going to festivals, standing up, doing a floor spot. Eventually someone said, 'Would you come to our club and we will give you some money?' That was actually how I started performing in a semi-professional way. But it was all done by word of mouth."

Let's pause for a moment and consider again the tableau of solo singing. Consider how daunting it is for the singer. For June. All those eyes watching her every move, hearts given in a sort of subliminal transaction, entrusting her with ferrying them on a narrative odyssey to a destination – a denouement – that won't disappoint. Hearts that want to be lifted, hearts that want to be broken. Minds scrutinising every inflection for flaws, ready and desperate to indulge themselves in a mocking jig of *schadenfreude*. You'd have to be a masochist to expose yourself like that, wouldn't you?

"I didn't say it was easy! But I did actually enjoy doing it. And it gives you a lot of freedom in terms of phrasing. There is a difference between accompanying yourself on an instrument – you know when you're going to sing the next bit – and having someone else accompany you. The art of accompaniment is extremely difficult. Good accompanists are very rare, because they have to think – they have to know exactly how you're thinking, because it isn't the same every time. That happens purely by working with someone and being on the same wavelength. If you try and graft it on to a kind of ad-hoc collaboration, it very seldom works."

¶

When June left home for Oxford University in 1966, and a place at St Hugh's College reading modern and medieval languages, her commitment to folk music became more conspicuous. She was appointed treasurer of the institution's Heritage Society, which once hosted a performance by Paul Simon, who earned a princely fee of £6.

"The Heritage Society was absolutely crucial," insists June. "On my first Saturday at Oxford there was something called the Freshers' Fair. All the university societies have little stalls. You go along and they try to entice you to join. I made a beeline for the folk club one. I wanted to join. I started going every Monday night in the upstairs room of The Bakers Arms in Jericho, a very working class area of Oxford. Little streets of thin terraced houses and pubs behind the Oxford University Press – 19th Century workers' housing.

"I immediately got into the social thing. We used to go to other pubs – always town pubs, not university pubs. Nice, ordinary places.

There was a big mix of musical interests. The club was for any town people who wanted to come as well, which was quite important. There were two very good Irish women singers, Toni and Anne, who had a good repertoire – songs I'd never heard before. There was a bluegrass trio, somebody played blues. It was expanding my musical knowledge through encountering people with different musical interests, but also the enthusiasm that people (who were) into traditional music had for seeking out songs, knowing where to look for them – printed sources, not just recordings. It widened how I experienced and found traditional music.

"One of the chaps, Hugh, who played the banjo, he had a 1930s hearse. The windscreen could fold half down – it was an amazing vehicle! We all used to pile in the back of that with instruments and go to a pub somewhere in the country. We'd be playing music on the way there, and playing when we got there. It was a remarkably good social mix. I played a lot of music, played a lot of darts. I used to play for the ladies' team in The Bakers Arms." Picture that, if you will – June Tabor as the folk music Trina Gulliver.

Oxford also brought her to national attention, or at least to the attention of the nation's eggheads who tuned into *University Challenge* in 1968. Captaining St Hugh's, she displayed "a disparity of primness between the Gitanes-smoking Tabor (hippy mane, short sleeves, chin resting on hand) and three teammates who appear to have been parachuted in from the 1950s".[25]

After completing her degree in the city of dreaming spires, June headed out for London and secured a job as a librarian in the borough of Hackney, which included Tottenham. This was years before she pledged her footy allegiance to near neighbours and fierce rivals Arsenal. She had worked in a library before university, and while there, between studying and singing.

"I was going to go to library school but I didn't get in," confesses June. "My tutor's report said that I was clever but not diligent, so they thought I wasn't serious about wanting to become a librarian, but I was actually. I love books, and a library gives you a degree of access to all kinds of things, not just music. To me, the only real work thing about working in a library, was having to get up and get there in the morning.

"I started on the counter, stamping books, and then eventually I got a more senior position: book purchasing, cataloguing, classification, subject enquiries, running a branch library, and all that sort of thing. But it's just the infinite variety of books passing through your hands, it really is heavenly. Tottenham library, which was part of the borough I worked for, had quite a good collection of records in the record library. They had *The Folk Songs Of Britain* on the Caedmon label, which was an American series put together from English field recordings. I put them on tape and photocopied the booklets. If I wanted to get hold of something, I found out and I knew how to do it. It was kind of incidental in a way."

Incidental but important in the maturation of June Tabor, folk singer.

Four

Folk Rock Babylon

♪

Pea soup, the Coronation, rationing and convent school "with nutty nuns" are some of Linda Thompson's earliest memories of London. It was after the Second World War, a time when the fortitude of capital dwellers – an attribute displayed in abundance as the Luftwaffe dropped bombs from on high during a sustained campaign between September 1940 and May 1941 – was needed once again as a post-conflict society endured terrible privation in rebuilding itself.

Linda Pettifer, as she was then, lived on a council estate in the north of the city until the age of 6. "My father was a bit of a dilettante, always losing every penny he had," she told *The Independent* newspaper in 2007. "He was exciting though. You'd be watching the only TV in the road and it would be carried out the front door as you watched it, by the repossession men. And irate punters knocking on the door after buying a car – 'There's no third gear!' You'd think it would be traumatising, but I actually found it funny."[26]

The family eventually moved to the Pettifer matriarch's native Glasgow. Linda fell hard for this hard place, "the city of the stare",[27] as novelist William McIlvanney described it.

"Glaswegians are droll and clannish – so am I," says Linda. "I loved the music too. Glasgow had a big influence on me musically. Listening to Alex Campbell, Hamish Imlach, The Fisher Family. And it gave me an abiding love of bagpipes!"

There was an aversion to anything English in the Pettifer household. It was "all about the Yanks",[28] Bing Crosby and Ray Charles, opposite ends of the sonic spectrum, being particular favourites.

Linda was always singing. It gave her a sense of empowerment. She went to parties – you could find a party almost anywhere in Glasgow those years – "where everyone got up and did a number". And the folk club scene was happening. "I sang with my friend, Izzy, a wonderful musician. He died of leukaemia when he was 20, which sort of coincided with my leaving for London. I was born there and always thought I'd go back when I was old enough."

London in the 1960s was unrecognisable from the London that had nurtured Linda Pettifer as a little girl. It positively swung. The world and his impossibly hip wife could be seen strutting down Carnaby Street. You wanted to hear some cool sounds? Head to the Marquee on Wardour Street, or the Troubadour on Old Brompton Road. You might catch The Rolling Stones, The Yardbirds or The Who, Bob Dylan or Paul Simon. This metropolis was switched-on, man.

Linda enrolled at LAMDA, the London Academy of Music and Dramatic Art, staying "until a teacher told me I'd be good at comedy – then I left".[29] Truth was, she couldn't stomach rejection and was "rubbish too". Rubbish at being a student or rubbish at being an actress? She doesn't say.

Changing her name from Pettifer to Peters, Linda became a regular at the coffeehouses, dominion of the folkies. "I lived near the Troubadour. I worked there as a waitress. Red Sullivan and Martin Windsor ran a great club there, and I started to sing the odd song *a cappella* or with other people who hung out there. My first professional gigs were done with a guy called Paul McNeill, a good traditional singer and a pretty good finger picker."

The duo recorded a brace of singles – a version of Dylan's "You Ain't Goin' Nowhere" on MGM and John D. Loudermilk's "You're Taking My Bag" on Larry Page's Page One – before going their separate ways. McNeill eventually quit the scene and settled in Fribourg, Switzerland, where he spent his later years as a busker until his death from cancer in 1989.

Martin Carthy, who knew McNeill well, remembers seeing him and Linda perform together, "and thinking, not only was she beautiful, but she couldn't half bloody sing. There was something really compelling about the way she sang. I love her as a woman and I love her singing. There's real depth to it. When somebody's got that extra depth, shit, what can you say?"

Linda continued to immerse herself in the folk revival, even if she wasn't conscious that she was part of any such thing. "You don't really feel like that when you're in the middle of it. I do remember I earned great money – £15 a gig. My rent was £6 a week. There were just millions of folk clubs all over Britain."

When not on stage herself, she got to hear Anne Briggs – "She was like the wild woman of Borneo to me" [30] – and Shirley Collins. American singer-songwriters like Phil Ochs, Tim Buckley and, of course, Dylan were around for a bit. They all played at the Troubadour or other of London's dingy basements.

"On a typical night (at the Troubadour) Sandy Denny would be there, or Annie Briggs, Bert Jansch, John Renbourn. Nick Drake sitting in the corner. Alan Lomax was around in those days too. Didn't stay open that late. Maybe one-ish, and then we would all go to people's flats,"[31] recalls Linda.

Linda actually dated Drake, though she suspected he was "probably gay and couldn't deal with it".[32] She also went out with Martin Carthy and Joe Boyd, a Harvard graduate who travelled throughout Europe as tour manager with Muddy Waters, Coleman Hawkins and Stan Getz, supervised Dylan's electric debut at Newport and opened London psychedelic ballroom UFO, before finding his niche as a producer.

To supplement her income as a singer on the folk circuit, Linda lent her voice to several TV advertising jingles. "Ski, the full of fitness food, and flour so fine it flows and flows," are a couple she recalls. "I did most of them with Manfred Mann. They were great fun and paid great money. Richard [Thompson] thought they were beneath me, so I stopped. I was a schmuck!"

¶

It's no coincidence that the three subjects of this book are women. Nor indeed that they emerged from the second folk revival in which women were every bit the talismanic equals of their gender opposites.

"The folk revival was on a small-ish scale, so it was something that women felt they could take on and then discovered they were good at it," says June Tabor. "If you're performing on the small scale of a folk club, you can gain confidence from that. An extremely important facet of the folk revival was that it gave all sorts of people, not just women, a place to learn how to sing to other people as opposed to just yourself. By no means are all women un-confident. But they can be a bit diffident sometimes about launching themselves. And this was a way to do it that gave them the confidence to do it a bit more."

What is curious though is that those women birthed by the movement were predominantly singers. "It was mostly men that played," says Maddy Prior. "Now I would say that's not true. There are much more women that play now. The balance has changed. That was one of the things about Bonnie Raitt – she could play the guitar properly, like a bloke! That made her different. Back then (during the revival) we tended to be figureheads. Girls are alright to be singers."

The ironic undertone of Maddy's last remark suggests that even in the folk idiom, men, bless them, weren't as right-on as they liked to believe. That they were still some way off working out the whole sexual parity thing. Frankie Armstrong, another singer to come out of that era, certainly thought this was the case. The folk clubs, she claimed, were "male chauvinist to a remarkable and remarkably unselfconscious degree".[33]

If Armstrong's assertion is true – and given the incremental advancement of social attitudes at the time, there's little reason to dispute it – the likes of Anne Briggs, Shirley Collins and Sandy Denny weren't inhibited by such sexism. Linda was a big fan of Denny's.

"She eclipsed everyone, I thought. Great timbre, great phrasing, great songs." The two first met when Denny was a trainee nurse at the Royal Brompton Hospital. "She used to come to London to sing. She was brilliant. She was my best friend,"[34] says Linda.

It was while at the Kingston College of Art that Denny began her folk apprenticeship. Down the road from the campus was an old barge moored on the River Thames. It had been converted into a folk club named, predictably, The Barge. It was here that she found her voice by singing from the floor.

Regularly acclaimed by critics as the doyenne of British folk rock, Karl Dallas wrote in a 1966 *Melody Maker* article that Denny "has the sort of rich soaring voice that could make her a British [Joan] Baez, though the comparison does her an injustice".[35] A year on, Dallas went even further, positing that "she has a sense of timing many would-be jazz singers would envy, which makes even the most tired old overdone folk lyric sound fresh and new".[36]

She was variously a member of The Strawbs, Fairport Convention and Fotheringay, before going it alone and releasing a quartet of albums between 1971 and 1977. Led Zeppelin were impressed enough by her to feature Denny on the untitled collection commonly known as *Led Zeppelin IV*, sharing vocals with Robert Plant on "The Battle Of Evermore".

Linda, speaking to John Harris in 2005, said, "I can remember Sandy saying to me, 'I'm going to try to write some songs'. And I thought to myself, 'That's ridiculous. She won't be able to do that'. We were young, and there weren't many women writing songs. And she played 'Who Knows Where The Time Goes', and I nearly fell off my chair.

"The thing that always amazed me about Sandy was that she thought she actually could appeal to the masses. Of course, she couldn't – and who would want to? If you're writing songs that people can shoot themselves to, you know you're not going to be in the charts. Sandy's music was uncomfortable. It demanded too much."[37]

The two "besties", as Linda refers to herself and Denny, only collaborated on one album, a 1972 project entitled *Rock On* by The Bunch, a collective also featuring Richard Thompson, Ashley Hutchings and Dave Mattacks, doing covers of rock'n'roll standards like "That'll Be the Day", "The Locomotion" and "When Will I Be

Loved?" Apparently the idea for the recording was hatched to test the newly-opened Manor Studios in Oxfordshire.

"The Bunch was quite significant," says Simon Nicol of Fairport Convention, "because that was the first time Richard and Linda were sort of banged up in the studio with a lot of other people. That's the first time you can hear him backing her voice."

It was, says Linda of her involvement, producer Trevor Lucas "who roped me in. He was a darling man."

The assembled throng worked hard and partied hard during the week-long sessions, a kind of "folk rock Babylon: Linda Peters recalled 'loads and loads of bedroom hopping' during the sessions; Thompson and Sandy Denny were throwing up in separate toilets while Trevor Lucas was recording 'The Locomotion'; and enough cans of beer were polished off that Lucas could knit an entire curtain of ring-pulls".[38]

Australian producer Lucas would later marry Denny, listed on the album's credits as "Britain's first lady of song, if you don't count Dorothy Squires".[39]

Tragically, Britain's first lady of song didn't enjoy anything like octogenarian Squires' longevity. Having left London for rural Northamptonshire in the mid-seventies, Denny gradually unravelled. Her marriage to Lucas hit the rocks, she was pregnant with daughter Georgia and enslaved to a cocaine habit.

Linda recalled, "I was worried when she was pregnant, because I knew she was doing drugs and drinking. And later on, she was crashing the car and leaving the baby in the pub and all sorts of stuff. I've said it before about Nick Drake – these days we might have done an intervention or something. But back then, you thought people would grow out of it."[40]

A 1977 tour to promote her album, *Rendezvous*, was the last time Denny would perform. Linda attended her London show, shocked by the haggard appearance of her friend, who had "blotches all over her face. She looked 50."[41]

The following year, Denny was dead at the age of 31 from what the coroner called traumatic mid-brain haemorrhage. She had fallen down stairs onto a stone floor while staying at her parents' Cornwall holiday cottage.

"It was horrible," Linda said in a 2004 interview with Steve Lafrenierc. "I rushed to the hospital and she was wrapped in a foil blanket to keep her body temperature up. She looked beautiful, not a mark on her. She never came around."[42]

— Five —

Two Couples And A Referee

♪

Steeleye Span may have been Ashley Hutchings' conception, but it became Maddy Prior's band. She was there in the beginning, and despite having exited the bus (to coin her analogy) on at least two separate occasions, there she remains. But the way Maddy tells it, she and Tim Hart only became part of the original line-up with Gay and Terry Woods through happenstance.

"Gay and Terry were staying with some friends of ours in the house we were living in. Ashley was trying to get a band together with Sweeney's Men and Gay, I think, originally. Sweeney's Men were in the process of breaking up, as I understand it. It finished up with Terry and Gay and Ashley. We were sitting round having dinner and they said, 'Do you want to join a band?' because we were in the room, really. We'd made a couple of albums, which was really unusual at the time. So we had a bit of kudos – we did traditional English folk. But we were just there."

The timing was perfect. Maddy and Tim "wanted to carry on working in traditional music, and we wanted to work in a rock band setting". They had done their time playing the folk clubs. "We'd sort of run out of steam. I'd stopped playing. Tim picked up the banjo and never put it down until he was better than me," says Maddy.

According to Rob Young in *Electric Eden: Unearthing Britain's Visionary Music*, Hutchings had Maddy and Tim in mind as early as June 1969, when he shared a ride with them back to London from the Keele Folk Festival. He had been part of Fairport Convention who, the same year, had literally electrified the folk revival with the seminal *Liege & Lief*, lauded by Maddy as "an album of traditional ballads sung by one of the most supple and emotive voices in Britain. Sandy Denny fronting Fairport inspired and infuriated us all. Driven by Ashley Hutchings' discovery of the potency of the material, and sustained by Richard Thompson's distinctive guitar, they had founded a corner stone on which a movement came to be rebuilt."

That movement was electric folk, where "phantoms of the agrarian past are channelled via an electrified present, chipping out the Anglo-paysan poetry of the countryside with blunt axes," says Dr Britta Sweers who traces the movement's origins to 1967, and the Davy Graham and Shirley Collins album *Folk Routes, New Routes*: "Folk rock, as such, basically started with *Liege & Lief*, yet also here we can observe slightly earlier first experiments that were recorded around 1968. I still really like the (Fairport) album, *What We Did On Our Holidays*, and especially the track, 'She Moves Through The Fair'. While some do not regard this as proper folk rock yet, or point out that Martin Lamble was maybe too shy to play his drums much louder, compared to Dave Mattacks, I nevertheless still like the very sensitive result. I always wished that Fairport would have tried out more of these approaches with a much more restrained electric/drum side. I always thought that these approaches had a much more vivid sound colour than later recordings. But this is probably also a matter of personal taste."

The plugged-in, amped-up version of folk was certainly not to the purists' taste.

"There was clearly a rejection," says Dr Sweers. Maddy claims it was "only a question of time before someone did it. Everyone wanted to be the one that did it. There was an element of, 'Bugger', going on amongst the performers. Some were a bit sneery about it. But the response generally was incredibly positive. People might have been mithering away in the corner, but my experience was that people were incredibly positive."

❡

When he left Fairport Convention, Hutchings felt a compulsion to throw himself further into traditional music. "It was far too soon to abandon it and I was very excited by this direction," he told John Tobler in 1991. "After we began performing the *Liege & Lief* material, I got to know a number of folk musicians and that gave me the confidence to form Steeleye Span."

Maddy is correct in recollecting that Hutchings wanted to establish a group with Irish outfit Sweeney's Men – alias Andy Irvine, Johnny Moynihan and Terry Woods – as well as Bob and Carole Pegg from Mr Fox. That came to nothing when Sweeney's Men dissolved – apparently Woods and Moynihan couldn't stand each other – and Irvine and Moynihan decided to go it alone. Enter Woods' wife Gay, along with Maddy and Tim. Hutchings had already bagged a record deal with RCA, and so the quintet adjourned to a rented bungalow in the Wiltshire village of Winterbourne Stoke, next door to Stonehenge, for three months.

"The winter was bitter, yet despite that, it was the start of something for me," Hutchings said of the period. "I recall lots of positive developments and the friendship. Really, a lot has been said about the squabbles and not enough about the good things in that line-up."

Ah yes, "the squabbles". Bit of a euphemism, that. True, Maddy and Gay spent the evenings step dancing and clog dancing, crocheting and embroidering, but beneath this pastoral atmosphere lurked something altogether more combustible, as the Anglo-Irish couples – polar opposites – became embroiled in a series of infantile spats.

"Was it a good fit? No, not really!" laughs Maddy all these years later. "It was two couples and a referee, really. We did alright, actually. And we made the album – which is lovely – before it all blew up. Terry and Gay just decided to leave. I think they assumed Ashley – Tyger, as he was at the time – would go with them. I don't think they ever got over the fact that he didn't. What goes on in other people's heads, I don't know."

Gay, who received an invitation to rejoin Steeleye Span when Maddy was having vocal problems, admitted to John O'Regan in

2000, "There were a lot of red-hot emotions in the past, but I am very grown up now and able to carry this stuff around. However, we are musicians and we do get flighty, but it goes with the territory. Looking back, I don't think they knew how to cope with me."

Martin Carthy lauds Gay as "an amazing singer", but adds, "By God, she doesn't half sow discord. I mean, she's lovely, but something happens there."

It couldn't last – and it didn't. *Hark! The Village Wait* was recorded at Sound Technique Studios in Chelsea, with Sandy Robertson (also the band's manager) producing. Gerry Conway and Dave Mattacks were drafted in on drums. Then the Woods quit, briefly joining Dr Strangely Strange before returning to Ireland.

Tim, reflecting on this period with John Tobler in 1994, explained, "Maddy and I were a clearly defined unit with our own ideas. Ashley had his ideas which Maddy and I agreed with, and Terry and Gay had their ideas, which tended to pull in a different direction, and after the first album was completed, there didn't seem much point in continuing, so Gay and Terry left."

Maddy, in the liner notes for the 1995 Chrysalis Records compilation, *Steeleye Span: Spanning The Years*, wrote, "The material on that album is particularly attractive, encompassing English and Irish songs, but unfortunately it was never able to be performed live.

"The strain of the rehearsal time spilt over into the recording situation and we parted on fighting terms at the end of the sessions. Everyone was very disappointed and there was pressure obviously from those outside the band who had invested time and money into the project. Then Tim came up with a stunning suggestion – 'Why not ask Martin Carthy to join?'"

❦

Carthy, a friend of Maddy and Tim's, had given Steeleye Span their name. It comes from the Lincolnshire ballad, "Horkstow Grange", the story of an argument between John Bowlin and Jon Span – the latter's nickname was Steeleye.

"I used to live in Warminster in Wiltshire. I was married to someone else. We had just moved down from London. When Tim and Maddy were on the road they would suddenly turn up, have a cup of tea in the afternoon and then go off and do a gig. They turned up one day and Tim said, 'We're going electric'. I thought that was interesting. There's a funny story about that. Maddy went to her mum and said, 'Mum, we're going electric'. And her mum said, 'Well, what are you going to do with that nice gas stove you have?'

"They were struggling to think of a name. I'd just been going a bit more into the Percy Grainger collection, and that's where I found the name Steeleye Span. Tim's ears pricked up and he wrote it down. They had a vote. There were three names up for it. Both the other names had something to do with waits – the old English country name for a band. Tim said that when it came to voting, he voted twice!

"It was a fantastic time. By that time Swarb [Dave Swarbrick] and I had split up, and so had my first wife and I. I must have been out on the road for three months. I went back to Warminster to visit our daughter, who would have been two and a half, a bit more. I had nowhere to live. I was basically living out of a suitcase – I had a case and a guitar. I was going around the country sleeping on people's sofas and stuff like that. I got back to Warminster and the phone rang. It was Tim. He said, 'Hi, Martin. Do you want to join Steeleye Span?' And I said, 'Yeah, alright'. It seemed like a good idea. I just fancied it. It was this huge thing – why not? Why would you say no to a thing like that?

"Swarb had asked me to join Fairport before that and I'd said no. It was a time when I really had to think. Swarb and I had basically been married for three and a half years. We relied on each other – or at least I relied on him – to an extent that I hadn't understood. So I had to completely rethink my repertoire. I was really quite excited. This would have been, in a sense, going back. It would have been doing what Swarb and I had done, only louder. My instinctive reaction was to say no, I didn't want to do this. What it produced was some great Fairport stuff. I really don't think I would have helped.

It wouldn't have helped me and it wouldn't have helped them in the long term. I always liked Maddy's singing and I thought Tim was fun. He had one or two interesting ideas, musically. It was worth a shot."

Carthy, says Maddy, gave Steeleye Span "a kind of stamp of approval. It legitimised it. It was exciting. It was one of the most challenging line-ups."

Joining Carthy in this second incarnation of Steeleye Span was violinist Peter Knight, who boasted "a classical background which had been subsequently overlaid with a strong Irish influence. He had worked hard at the music and become known in all the Irish music pubs in London."

Maddy and Tim, together with Hutchings, Carthy and Knight, made two albums – *Please To See The King*, which scaled the British Top 50, and *Ten Man Mop, Or Mr Reservoir Butler Rides Again*, and appeared as musicians and actors at London's Royal Court Theatre in Keith Dewhurst's *Pirates And Corunna*, as well as providing the soundtrack for a stage adaptation of Robert Louis Stevenson's *Kidnapped* at the Lyceum in Edinburgh.

Steeleye Span's involvement in theatre came about when they gave a concert at the Royal Court in October 1970. Dewhurst was in the audience that night, along with the venue's staff director Bill Bryden. The pair had originally approached Martin Carthy to contribute the music to *Pirates*, but he was busy on other projects. Maddy, together with Tim and Knight, drove overnight from Sunderland to rehearse the production the next morning. Dewhurst was sufficiently impressed to script an entire play around Steeleye Span.

Ostensibly, *Corunna* told the story of soldiers and camp followers travelling across Spain during the Napoleonic Wars. Hutchings narrated, Knight was a soldier whose tongue had been pulled out and who could only communicate by playing the violin, Carthy a soldier left behind to face the French horsemen and Maddy a camp follower. But essentially, the drama was about the misery of warfare. It ran at the Royal Court for a week before touring the country.

Potential disaster was offset by comedy improvisation in Harrogate. The first act ended with sound effects of galloping horses over which Steeleye Span shouted, "It's the French horsemen, let's move!" But on this occasion the sound effects tape had been mysteriously replaced by one featuring organ music. The awkwardness of the situation was relieved when someone quipped, "It's the French organists, let's move!"

It was around this period when Mac MacLeod – who had returned to the UK in 1968 after living in both Stockholm and Copenhagen – saw Maddy performing with Steeleye Span for the first time.

"Very impressive," he exults. "Maddy always had a wonderful voice, but now here she was showing that all those hours dancing in the jazz club were coming to good use. A great mover, she was using the whole stage and really knew how to project and connect with the audience. Yes, once again a natural progression, and Maddy took to it like a fish to water."

§

By 1971, the restless Hutchings was moving on again, soon followed by Carthy. Maddy insists she still can't fathom the reasons for Hutchings' departure. "I was a bit surprised he left. I still don't really know why he left. I don't think he probably knows why he left. It was a case of, 'Have we got a band?' at the time."

Yet she said to John Tobler in 1995 that "there undoubtedly were strains building up. Talk of touring America was uncomfortable for Ashley. He didn't want to fly, but I suspect the project had run its course for him."

For Tim, it was a combination of Hutchings' aversion to touring America, and the fact that he "basically didn't want to do what Martin and Maddy and I wanted to do. In some ways, Martin, Maddy and I were quite close – we'd all worked the folk clubs. We had the same roots and the same attitude towards the music, which was somewhat more robust than Ashley, who had a very precious attitude towards traditional music at the time, and regarded it as a quaint art form, whereas we'd all been working with it for years. We found this attitude very curious – this rocker who thought it was a fragile thing. It's lasted for hundreds of years – it doesn't matter what you do with it, because it's going to outlast you anyway."

Bob Johnson and Rick Kemp then joined, the latter believing that Carthy was still in the band. "He didn't know until the first day," says Maddy. "Bob and Rick were both rockers. They brought the rock element in. And Bob, of course, brought the big structured ballads in."

If Kemp was disappointed that Carthy was no longer a member of Steeleye Span, he would have been crestfallen by what Rob Young identified as the trigger for Carthy's departure, allegedly because "he objected to Hart and Prior's desire to replace Hutchings with bassist Rick Kemp".

Carthy himself finally sets the record straight: "When Ashley announced that he was going to go – because he decided that the band had become too Irish – we had quite a hefty discussion about what we were going to do afterwards. I said that we could do with being a little more English rather than ersatz Irish. I suggested that we asked John Kirkpatrick. Everybody else said, 'No, let's just get another bass player'. There was another bass player in the offing, who was Rick Kemp. I had nothing against Rick – he was a lovely bloke, still is. We couldn't resolve it. So I sort of decided that it would be better if I left. I was really heartbroken at the thought of leaving, because I'd had such a good time and I'd learnt so much. Speaking selfishly and personally, it taught me how to play less.

"We were a good band. The reason I left was, we'd been a five-piece band, we'd gone down to four. Three people thought we should go one way, but one person thought we should go another way. So the thing to do was let the one person who disagreed go, and let him get on with it. I told the manager and left the office feeling this huge weight off my shoulders. It was really weird. I was dreading it. I didn't want to do it. And then I went and did it and immediately felt better."

Kemp had a chequered curriculum vitae. At the age of 12, he won the England Skiffle Competition at the Cafe de Paris in London, and later played with several local bands in Hull, was in demand as a session bassist, embellished his reputation in the 1960s alongside singer-songwriter Michael Chapman and had a brief stint in King Crimson. Johnson, meanwhile, came from a rock'n'roll background, having worked with Gary Glitter when the latter was known as Paul Raven.

Carthy may have gone, but he would be back. His involvement in the early gestation of Steeleye Span had "a major impact on the group. He was not only a prolific source of material, but he also gave the group more security in handling the material."

They were about to bring that material to vast audiences beyond their imaginings.

Six

A Crack Den With Fancy Curtains

♪

Fairport Convention were a covers band when Joe Boyd first saw them live. They played American music – Bob Dylan, Leonard Cohen, Richard Fariña – in an Anglicised West Coast style. There was nothing particularly special about them. Not then. But the 18-year-old guitarist with the shaggy hair captivated Boyd's attention. He did a solo quoting from Django Reinhardt and Charlie Christian. Impressively precocious: enough for Boyd to barge into the dressing room afterwards and ask if they wanted to cut a record.

The guitarist was Richard Thompson. He could, Boyd wrote in his memoir, *White Bicycles: Making Music In The 1960s*, "imitate almost any style, and often does, but is instantly identifiable. In his playing you can hear the evocation of the Scottish piper's drone and the melody of the chanter, as well as echoes of Barney Kessel's and James Burton's guitars and Jerry Lee Lewis' piano. But no blues clichés."

When Boyd became involved with Fairport Convention, Thompson, embarrassed that they were still rehashing other people's material, began to write songs for the band. His immense contributions to their oeuvre included "Meet On The Ledge", "Genesis Hall" and "Crazy Man Michael", a two-hander with Dave Swarbrick. But Thompson was never going to stick around, even if his eventual departure in 1971, after the *Full House* album and subsequent American tour, was impulsive rather than intended.

"I left Fairport as a gut reaction and didn't really know what I was doing, except writing. I was writing stuff and it seemed interesting and I thought it would be fun to make a record. And at the same time I was doing a lot of session work as a way of avoiding any serious ideas about a career," Thompson told Patrick Humphries.

Within a year, he had issued his debut solo album, *Henry The Human Fly*, "an attempt to create an English form of rock'n'roll by blending elements of English traditional music with American rock". Backing vocalist on a couple of tracks, "Shaky Nancy" and "The Angels Took My Racehorse Away", was one Linda Peters, introduced to Thompson by their mutual friend, Sandy Denny.

"The first time I remember talking to him was at a Chinese restaurant on the King's Road. I had never met a vegetarian before. Sandy thought he was the bee's knees, so I was keen to find out why," says Linda.

To *The Independent* in 2007, she remembered him as "a very intense young man, and I was a flibbertigibbet. And you know how that goes."

How it went was the intense young man and the flibbertigibbet got together. Simon Nicol, Richard's former Fairport Convention bandmate, had known Linda as "a sort of mate of Sandy's, though not bosom buddies – they weren't inseparable, but she was in that circle as a sort of jobbing singer. They knew people in common as well. But that wasn't really the kind of orbit that I moved in personally. Obviously we crossed orbits when the band was involved.

"Linda was striking and there was something elementally different about her from her predecessors in that role on his arm. She seemed a very confident match for Richard, because confidence wasn't his strongest point. At the time he had quite a bit more of a stammer than you're aware of these days in conversation, and he tended to keep his eyes down on the floor when he was playing, that sort of thing. But that was just an age thing. But she had the sort of extrovert confidence he was lacking. She was very animated, not stupidly, boisterously extroverted, but somebody with a definite sense of their place in the world.

"The singing seemed to come later. I only saw her when she was off duty, and she didn't burst into song when we were all sitting around. I was more aware of her as a social companion in restaurants and things like that. Obviously the closer they became to each other, the less time they spent with us."

Richard and Linda married following what the red tops might have called a whirlwind romance. They threw their lot in together professionally as well as personally, touring the folk clubs as two thirds of a trio – Hokey Pokey – with Simon Nicol.

"We just fell into this thing of doing a folk club and small college thing," says Nicol. "We'd all sit down, because Richard was playing a pedal-operated keyboard kind of thing, so he had to sit down. They just wanted an extra guitarist, I suppose, to flesh it out a bit. We largely did his songs, but he would throw in the odd Hank Williams song, and occasionally do Chuck Berry stuff on the two guitars. It was a triangle, but he was definitely the musical leader. It was a very jolly little thing."

Then Jo Lustig came along. The American entrepreneur had, in the parlance of an industry that prides itself, rather bumptiously, on possessing considerably more perception than it actually does, discovered Pentangle. He also managed Ralph McTell and would go on to oversee the affairs of Steeleye Span during their halcyon Chrysalis period. Lustig signed Richard and Linda as a duo.

¶

Almost before the contractual ink was dry, Richard and Linda Thompson – for that was the appellation bestowed upon them – set about their first album. *I Want To See The Bright Lights Tonight* was recorded on a shoestring budget – £2,500 – over three days in May 1973, at Sound Techniques in London. According to Rob Young in *Electric Eden: Unearthing Britain's Visionary Music*, because of a vinyl shortage caused by the global oil crisis, the record didn't arrive on the shelves until nearly a year later. Richard told a different tale to Mat Snow. "Island hated it," he stated. "It was only acclaimed in retrospect. When you make records you don't think, 'Gosh, we're making history here, a classic'. If you've got any sense anyway."

Richard wrote all ten songs and, in addition to guitar, played hammered dulcimer, mandolin, whistle, piano, electric piano and harmonium. Simon Nicol, Pat Donaldson, John Kirkpatrick, Trevor Lucas and Manchester brass outfit, The CWS Silver Band, were among those musicians who rounded out the beautiful noise.

"I liked the sound of Linda's voice in "Withered And Died". It's such a sad song. Why do I love it so?" wonders Ann Savoy, musician, author, photographer and producer of the Grammy Award-nominated, *Evangeline Made: A Tribute To Cajun Music*, on which both Richard and Linda guest (separately), alongside Linda Ronstadt, Maria McKee and Rodney Crowell.

"'Down Where The Drunkards Roll', I love the dulcimer in it as it plays against her voice – there is this drone thing between them. I love her voice with Richard's low harmony. I love all the descriptions in the song – the boys in green velvet with silver buckles, the perfect description of the way a drunk sees himself/herself."

Richard and Linda made six albums together. But it's the two bookending their combined output, *I Want To See The Bright Lights Tonight* and 1982's *Shoot Out The Lights*, that endure as landmark documents. Albums such as *Hokey Pokey* and *Pour Down Like Silver*, while they struggled "with a sense of hard-won knowledge, a literal disillusionment, a shattering of the rosy lens" (*Electric Eden* – Rob Young), pale by comparison some four decades on. But as Richard acknowledged to Colin Irwin, "you're bound to make a few bummers".[43]

For most of that period, Richard and Linda were engaged on a spiritual as much as musical journey, which could be cited as a mitigating factor in the creation of said bummers. Or at least Richard was engaged on a spiritual journey – Linda "just went along with it". Apparently, following a chat with Ian Whiteman, former pianist with The Action and Mighty Baby, and a visit to a religious meeting on Euston Road in London, they found Islam. Well, Sufism, to be exact, "the inner, mystical or psycho-spiritual dimension of Islam".[44] Also defined as "a school for the actualisation of divine ethics. It involves an enlightened inner being, not intellectual proof; revelation and witnessing, not logic."[45] The Sufi is "a lover of God, and like any other lover, he proves his love by constant remembrance of the Beloved".[46] This has a dual effect, inward and outward. The inward effect "is that the Sufi's remembrance distances himself from the domain of 'I and you' and joins him with the realm of unity",[47] while the outward is the manifestation of God's attributes in the Sufi's conduct.

The Thompsons, impelled by Richard's utter conviction, relinquished their capacious abode in leafy Hampstead, shed all material possessions and took up residence in a Maida Vale commune.

"I hated the commune," Linda admits. "Now I don't even have people over – I like to be on my own. It was detrimental to my life, that's for sure, though in retrospect I learned some stuff. Namely, if you're an over-educated white person yearning for more than materialism can give you, get over it.

"Richard was more detached than Stevie Wonder's retina, as I like to say. Men and women were separated in the commune. Needless to say the women had to look after the kids. I didn't have the strength to leave. Well, I did once, but went back."

She was more forthcoming about the experience in a 2013 conversation with Tim Cummings.

I think in a commune – and it was very much that kind of commune – they have to break your spirit. They'd wake you up in the middle of the night. It's a bit like being in the army. It wasn't good for me. And I hate to say it, and I've never said it in my life before, but Richard's a good man, but he was not good for me. That whole lifestyle just wasn't good for me. It shook me up. But I did learn some good things. I can sit in traffic jams for hours. I just don't care about that stuff. Or stand in queues. I love queuing. It's very therapeutic. So I learnt a certain "Don't sweat the small stuff", but it wasn't good. Everybody was meant to bring up everyone else's kids, so all the kids were neglected. And if you paid too much attention to your own kids, they'd say, "You've got to pay as much attention to Johnny as your own child", and it just didn't work for me. And I don't think it was good for my kids at all. I really don't.

She likened the commune to a crack den with fancy curtains.

If you walked into a crack den, as I've done in New York, you'd think, "This is exactly the same as a commune". We had prayer and

MADDY

Top left: Maddy and Daddy. Allan Prior was a successful TV script writer. (*Rex/Ling/Evening News*)

Top right: Steeleye Span hanging out, literally! Peter Knight, Maddy, Tim Hart, Rick Kemp. (*Photographer unknown. Image courtesy of John Dagnell/Park Records*)

Above: Steeleye Span January 1971, in rehearsals for *Please To See The King*. L–R: Maddy, Peter Knight, Ashley Hutchings, Tim Hart and Martin Carthy. (*Estate Of Keith Morris/Getty Images*)

Three different aspects of Maddy from the 1970s.
(*Photographers Unknown. Images courtesy of John Dagnell/Park Records*)

The Silly Sisters in 1976 and also at the 1989 Bracknell Festival,
where June is looking very 1980s! (*Estate Of Keith Morris/Getty Images*)
and (*Unknown photographer. Image courtesy of June Tabor*)

Maddy at the Concert Hall Reading, December 2011.
(*Andrew Spiers/Alamy*)

deprivation, they've got crack. But it's the same thing. And they all look the same, with the same longing and the same desperation.[48]

In a 1988 interview, Richard explained that, at the time of his conversion, he was "just a young person trying to connect with reality somehow. I just realised that Sufism was where it was at. Intellectually I decided it was the thing to do, and when I met Muslims I recognised a quality in them that I wanted in myself."[49]

When it wasn't interfering with their music – Richard's Mullah forbade him to play the electric guitar, and religious commitments kept them off the road for three years – Sufism was infiltrating it. Check out the sleeve of *Pour Down Like Silver*, Richard's head wrapped in a turban, Linda looking out from beneath a headscarf. The plan at one stage was to abandon what it was that constituted their career – they even became antique dealers for a spell.

"I wanted to see if I could do anything else," Richard said. "Getting away from music helped me to understand the reasons I do it, and told me that I am a musician, that's where my talent lies and that's what I should do."[50]

§

After the Sufism adventure (or ordeal, if you're Linda), there were another two albums as a duo and an American tour that "has gone down in the rock annals as a legendarily bitter and destructive undertaking",[51] before marital and artistic relationships were dissolved. The final album, *Shoot Out The Lights*, was produced by Richard's ex-Fairport manager and Linda's ex-fiancé, Joe Boyd, "live in three days". The songs that feature on the set had already been recorded a year previously at Chipping Norton Studios in Oxfordshire, with Gerry Rafferty and his producer, Hugh Murphy, at the helm. Rafferty actually financed the project himself and ended up losing some £30,000 when it was shelved.

Simon Nicol found the second sessions recording "a little bit odd because we'd already made one version of that album in a different environment, with different people and a very different sounding view. That was the sound Richard decided, very early on in the process, was not where he wanted to go. I quite liked it, but in retrospect it was a sweeter sounding but emasculated version of what came later, which is a record that has certainly stood the test of time."

He remembers Linda as "a definite presence in the studio. In a strange way, she and Richard and Joe were the sort of ruling triangle. We were all sort of subject to their joint instruction. Linda was never not interested. It wasn't a case of, 'OK, I haven't got anything to do until this evening, when I come back and put some vocals on, so I'm going to bugger off to the shops'. She was there sitting on the sofa reading a paper, making the tea or just generally cheering people up."

The songs on *Shoot Out The Lights* are, according to *Rolling Stone*, "crystal clear portraits of dissolving relationships, cast with wronged or dissatisfied lovers on the one hand, and riveting tales of death and violence on the other".[52] But Richard dismissed the notion that the lyrics presage the eventual failure of his and Linda's marriage.

"The theorists can theorise, and they may be right, but from a practical point of view, for myself, it was just the stuff that I was writing, and it didn't bear any relationship to life as I could see it at the time."[53]

Linda disagreed, claiming "a cohesion to all those songs that was part of what was going on at the time. We gravitated to that kind of subject matter. There was a kind of common denominator in those songs – they fit together, and we weeded them out that way. The common denominator was utter misery. It was kind of a subliminal thing, but that was definitely it. I think we both were miserable and didn't quite know how to get it out. I think that's why the album is so good – we couldn't talk to each other, so we just did it on record."[54]

Linda told *Rolling Stone* magazine she couldn't understand why people liked *Shoot Out The Lights*. The songs, she conceded, were good, but the performances far from outstanding. Still she reckoned it was her and Richard's *magnum opus*.

"People are often really horrified to hear me say, 'I do wish in a way that I was going through that again'. They say, 'But you were mad and demented and ill!' And I say, 'Yeah, but I really could sing good'. So there's an upswing, even in that darkest moment'."[55]

Boyd, who was his "usual self as producer, commenting, cajoling, encouraging", reckons the songs "sound as if Richard wrote them about the break-up, but it may have been unconscious. There was tension in the studio, but they were together."

❡

But not for much longer. Richard fell for someone else – Nancy Covey, his wife since 1985 – and left the family home when Linda was pregnant with their daughter, Kamila, in 1982. The woman scorned took revenge of sorts on a notorious US tour. Fuelled on vodka and anti-depressants ("I had to get slaughtered to get through it"[56]), Linda would trip Richard up as they emerged onstage, and then slag him off during the gigs.

"I was a monster. It was like a Chekhov play," she reflected in 1985. But, as she points out for this book, "Nobody wanted me to go. So, I went. It was a tad harrowing. And antagonistic, on my part, certainly."[57]

The roll call of ignominy also involved a car theft, an arrest and a disappearing act in Los Angeles, where a very drunk Linda was hauled out of the gutter by Linda Ronstadt, who then brought her home for a day and a half of recuperation.

In *Richard Thompson – Strange Affair: The Biography*, Richard admitted to Patrick Humphries that going on the tour was stupid.

"The marriage was basically over, and going on tour with someone you've just broken up with and are not getting on with terribly well, was a disastrous idea."

Simon Nicol recalls that the worst thing about it was its unpredictability. "It's the madness of it. Every time you bumped into somebody and had time away from them, you didn't know how they were going to be. Jo Lustig wasn't much help as a peacekeeper.

Linda was absolutely like a firework, a completely out of control thing. Other days she'd be dosed up on something or other and she'd be just glazed and singing. There were mad things like getting the bags off a carousel at an airport and realising that Linda wasn't anywhere to be seen and the hire car had gone, that she'd driven off into the dark in Albuquerque or somewhere.

"Dave Mattacks, Pete Zorn and I were the sort of three musketeers, we called ourselves. We were sort of having to huddle together for mutual self protection, just trying to keep our heads down and play the music as well as we could in the circumstances. I loved the material. The crowds were very into it, very excited by it. It brought the songs into sharp focus, lyrically. Inevitably you'd start to think, 'What's he saying here? Is this to be taken literally? And when did he write this song? How many months ago did these thoughts form in his head?'

"I thought she got through it and I was very glad she got through it, but it was killing her. The only good thing about it was that you knew there was a diary attached to it, and it did have to run its course. And every day you did was a day nearer the end of it. We were in Los Angeles and we got on a plane. We had to get off the plane in San Francisco, there was like an hour-long break while they reloaded the transatlantic folk. When it was time to get back on the plane she disappeared again. She was sitting within sight of me and her seat was empty. They shut the doors and pushed the plane back and we looked at each other and thought, 'Oh, God, what a mess she's got herself into', because she was the only one of the party missing. And then as we were taxying out towards the runway they came over the PA and said, 'We've realised that we've left some important foodstuffs behind, so we're just returning to the terminal to get that trolley on board'. And we went back to the terminal, which I think is absolutely unheard of on a 747 embarking on a ten hour flight to London. The door opened and on she got. I can only imagine the fuss she must have made at the gate."

A truly wretched denouement to an alliance that neither party, along with the rest of us – perhaps because of the innate human fascination with the tragedy of other people's lives – seem fully able to quit. Novelist Nick Hornby had, at one stage, even embarked on a film script dealing with the very public disintegration of the Thompsons' relationship, before aborting the idea. But it's the music they made together that has endured as their legacy.

"Richard wasn't confident as a singer, and Linda was a wonderful singer who loved his songs," says Joe Boyd. "He had the expertise, I had a pretty voice and a lot of feeling," is Linda's assessment of why she and Richard were such a perfect fit, at least when wedded in song.

Their son, Teddy, reckons it's "a nebulous thing to know why two voices work together, unless you're related. But actually, now that I'm saying this out loud, I'm not so sure that their voices had a particular blend that was really heart-wrenching, like a blend of harmonies. I think they both had very individual voices. So it wasn't necessarily that kind of glue that they had, that magic thing. My mum had a very pure, angelic kind of voice. And my dad had a quite sinister thing to him, in his voice and in his playing, quite dark. My mum was singing dark music but she had a pretty voice, a pure voice – a virginal voice, I would say, when she was young. So maybe it was that meeting of the good and the evil."

Seven

Elf City

*

The third incarnation of Steeleye Span was "a true fusion of styles",[58] a sonic transformation – with its concomitant potential for striking commercial gold – that aroused the interest of Chrysalis, then a relatively small but growing label. Their faith in the band was soon vindicated, if somewhat unexpectedly, when "Gaudete", a Latin chant thought to have originated in the 16th Century, became an unlikely hit single in the British charts, peaking at No.14 in 1973. Bob Johnson had heard the song while attending a folk carol service with his father-in-law in Cambridge.

Steeleye Span were pushing the boundaries not just of their folk roots, which seemed at a very distant remove, but of their electric folk persona – boundaries that were completely obliterated with the assimilation of mummers' plays and "The Lyke Wake Dirge" into their live act.

Mummers were masked individuals who, during winter festivals in Europe, paraded the streets and entered houses to either dance or play dice in absolute silence. The play is predicated on "the story of St George and the Seven Champions of Christendom",[59] in which the saint, introduced as a gallant Christian hero, fights an infidel knight, at the end of which combat one of them is slain. At this juncture, a doctor "restores the dead warrior to life. Other characters include a presenter, a fool in cap and bells, and a man dressed in woman's clothes. Father Christmas also appears. It is likely that the basic story of death and resurrection was grafted onto an older game that stemmed from primitive ritual."[60]

Elf City

The title of "The Lyke Wake Dirge", or lamentation, makes reference to the vigil maintained over the deceased between death and burial, known as the wake – "lyke" is an obsolete word for corpse, derived from the German "leiche" and the Dutch "lijk". The performance of the piece, during which the group were draped in cassocks, made for quite a spooky spectacle. It scared the shit out of American audiences when they crossed the Atlantic as support to Jethro Tull in 1973, and was in contrast to the Steeleye Span who, a year previously, had backed Procol Harum Stateside.

"Procol Harum were a bit pissed off with us really, because their audience were all booze and downers, and we came on all jolly," says Maddy. "They didn't take it terribly well, although they were fairly gracious about it. We were just... hysterical, I think is the best way to describe it. It was an amazing experience to play America, and then to go out with Jethro playing stadiums was just ridiculous.

"Their audiences were perplexed by us, probably more than anything. We opened with 'The Lake Wyke Dirge', wearing mummers' ribbons with very tall hats. They floodlit us underneath, creating shadows behind us. It freaked half the audience out. We put these tall hats on and put the ribbons over our faces. It was a pretty extraordinary image. I spent the whole of rehearsals sticking these blessed things on cassocks that we got from Tim's dad. Our poor tour manager, Chris Coates, had to stand there while I was doing this."

It was Maddy who came up with the idea – the other members of Steeleye Span resisted fiercely at first. "They said, 'Well, if it goes wrong, we're going to mess about and send it up'. I was really cross! But when we got on stage and they put these lights up – I didn't know they were going to do that – the whole audience just went still. The band were transfixed. Then the drums started up and I went into a dance with the ribbons and everything. It was an amazing opening of a show. I think I changed outfits about five times in the set. It was very much a visual show. And then, afterwards, we did an actual mummers' play at one point. We did a sword dance – all sorts of stuff – and I got into the dancing and threw myself about a lot. It was very different.

"The light show then was part of the deal. Obviously we would have some access to reasonable lighting, though not what Jethro had. It was like it is now, a big part of the show. On the tour we did with Jethro, they had *A Passion Play* [a short film] with the projector going. So the whole show was very visual."

¶

Steeleye Span and Jethro Tull had been "friendly in a mate-ish sort of way", Tull frontman Ian Anderson recalls. Theirs was "not a musical bond, *per se*" as Jethro Tull "had little to do with folk at the time. We were professionally joined at the hip but stylistically miles apart."

On that American tour, according to Anderson, the two camps became "kindred spirits on stages far from home. Peter Knight was a man's man, and Tim Hart the thoughtful, intense performer. Maddy - a stately lady with a great stage presence and huge authority regarding the history of British folk music – was the slightly separate soul through the inevitable gender requirements of road life.

"It was tough for them being a generic UK folk band and playing to US rock audiences in the heyday of sex, drugs and rock'n'roll. But they made a good impact and earned much respect. Even in the arenas and acoustically messy places we had to try to fill."

After returning to Britain, Steeleye Span invited Anderson to help them out as production consultant on their next album, *Now We Are Six*. By his own admission, his was a nominal role.

"They had complete tracks of all but two songs. I got David Bowie to play saxophone on a track ('To Know Him Is To Love Him') and we re-recorded 'Thomas The Rhymer' in a more poppy way. Mostly it was a mixing job."

Maddy, writing in the sleeve notes for *Steeleye Span: Spanning The Years*, claimed Rick Kemp "had known David and Mick Ronson in Hull and asked through a friend if he would come and play. He duly obliged and we passed an interesting afternoon watching David and Ian gently sparring."[61]

The following year's *Commoners Crown* featured a guest appearance by another luminary, this time from the world of comedy.

"While sitting over lunch we were discussing what we need to sparkle up the track, 'New York Girls', Maddy told John Tobler. "'Ukulele would be good', someone said. 'Anyone got one? Anybody know someone who can play one?' 'Peter Sellers plays it', says Bob. Pause. Eyes meet. 'Why not? We could ask. He could only say no'.

"So we spent another interesting afternoon with a rather diffident Peter Sellers. I don't think he'd ever been asked to play on a session before and was apprehensive about the whole affair until he realised we were delighted to have him there. He loosened up as time went by and finally finished by adding, unprompted, some Goon voices. We were ecstatic."[62]

Bowie and Sellers tended to have a coquettish rather than wholly consummated relationship with the mainstream at this stage of their careers. They possessed an allegiance to their artistry that prevented them from flagrantly flogging it in the marketplace, and an eccentric bent that allowed their respective dalliances with Steeleye Span. Put another way, neither collaboration was quite as daft as it may have seemed. The same, however, could not be said for Mike Batt's involvement on the band's next two albums, *All Around My Hat* and *Rocket Cottage*. Batt was a former in-house songwriter and head of A&R at Liberty Records, responsible for signing and producing The Groundhogs' debut, *Scratching The Surface*. He also fronted The Mike Batt Orchestra. But it was for a bunch of fictional furry creatures – Orinoco, Wellington, Tomsk, Bungo, Tobermory, Madame Cholet and Great Uncle Bulgaria – that he lodged his name in the consciousness of the British public. The Wombles were a novelty pop outfit featuring musicians, including Batt himself alongside Chris Spedding, Ray Cooper and Clem Cattini, among others, dressed as characters from the children's TV show based on a book series by Elisabeth Beresford. They had hits with such instantly forgettable yet infuriatingly memorable singles as "The Wombling Song", "Remember You're A Womble" and "Banana Rock".

"It was The Wombles that turned me on to Mike," said Tim Hart in 1994. "I listened to an album out of silliness really, and I couldn't believe the production, because it was brilliant on each track, and each track was totally different – I thought, 'This is the producer we've been looking for'. Chrysalis wanted us to find a producer, and we talked to various famous producers who wanted to stamp their production technique on our music, but that wasn't what we were about. Mike was the sort of guy who could come in and actually adapt to what we were doing and try to understand it and contribute and work with us."[63]

Martin Carthy acknowledged Batt's prowess in the studio. "Whatever you thought of The Wombles musically, as a piece of production it was bloody brilliant," he told me.

It's fair to say that when Tim proposed Batt as producer of *All Around My Hat*, the rest of Steeleye Span were not amused.

Says Maddy, "Tim just said, 'I know you're going to laugh, but this guy's a really good producer. These songs are great and he's produced them beautifully'. So we had a listen, very doubtfully, and we said, 'Yeah, actually you're right, it is good'.

"We thought it would be an interesting combination. We always liked to do slightly odd things. We'd always go outside the folk world, go somewhere that was unexpected, like getting Peter Sellers in and David Bowie. He [Batt] thought we were a bit odd, I think, at first. He didn't get the music, but he sort of understood bits of it. There were bits of it that perplexed him. But he brought a great pop sensibility to it. He did a lovely arrangement on 'Cadgwith Anthem'. He just sort of brought that other head in, if you like, which was great for us. We'd been to America by then and we were sort of up for having a good time."

Batt himself was perplexed when Tim approached him. "I got this call out of the blue. He asked if I'd be interested in producing Steeleye. I went for a pint with him and Peter Knight. I wasn't lacking in self esteem as a producer, but it still bemused me as to why they would pick me. They said it was because they loved The Wombles drum sounds. I thought, 'Fair enough, that's a good enough reason'. It was at the time they'd been going through some quite imaginative choices.

"I knew the single, 'Gaudete' – I'd seen them do it on telly. I knew of the band, of course, because I was into the music. I wasn't a folk fan, although I used to do folk clubs when I was young. I used to go to pubs where there were folk singers, and I'd sometimes get on the piano and that sort of thing. But I wasn't a folkie."

It was Batt who oversaw Steeleye Span's only foray into the upper reaches of the singles chart with "All Around My Hat", which made No. 5 in 1975, though he prefers to underplay his part in its success. "The first time I heard anything full frontal was when I went to a rehearsal studio where they were working, to meet them all – the ones I hadn't met. I heard them working on 'All Around My Hat'. They already had that shuffle rhythm going on and a violin opening, not unlike 'Remember You're A Womble'. A lot of people thought I walked in and said, 'Oh yeah, you should have an opening like "Remember You're A Womble"', but I didn't. They may have taken it from the idea, I don't know – I'd be flattered if they did. I might have made some suggestions about changing the routine of it, so that maybe we went to the middle eight quicker, or maybe I brought in the idea of dropping out near the end, making it acoustic for a moment before the drums came back in. The way I record a band who are already great at harmonies, would be to record them all in mono, or on a pair of stereo mics at the same time. A lot of people would just record the lead singer and then add the harmonies on. With a band like Steeleye, who were so good at harmonies, I would just clean it up afterwards, tart it up, fatten it up, by adding on overdubs on top.

"'All Around My Hat' was such an unusual subject. Hit singles are usually about love. The actual record was so exciting to be part of –– you knew you were onto something good. There have been times in my life where I've been involved with certain records and have just known they were going to be a smash. 'Bright Eyes' was one of them. I didn't know this would necessarily be a defining single for the band, but I just knew it was something highly original they had created and that we had made a powerful record of it. And if anything, I helped to provide the power, weirdly. I came in as a sort of wondering Womble, wondering why I was there, and one would think, 'Well, what would he add?' They already had a powerful rhythm section. One of the things I think I did help to do was to present that power by recording it in a way that was punchy and well recorded and hopefully imaginatively arranged."

"All Around My Hat" was an amalgam of the 18th century song of the same name – which Maddy had heard from Tony Foxworthy – and another song, "Farewell He".

"I liked it but I didn't like the words," she says. "So I put the words from another song to it, which makes absolutely no sense whatever, but they're both traditional songs stuck together. I kept the chorus. Then I just took it in and said to the band, 'What about this?' Once they put that track behind it, I thought, 'This is great'.

"People came in with specific things, everyone kind of threw something in – especially at that time. Rick and Bob were both very creative with riffs. They were the rock element. Pete and I were folkier. And Tim was somewhere between the two. I just liked dancing to it.

"I think of it as our sort of anthem. It's our signature. I don't mind that, because it's still a bloody hard song to sing. It's in a hard key. It requires a lot of energy to sing it. You can't sit back and sing it sweetly. You've got to put everything into it. I don't mind it at all. It's still a challenging song as far as I'm concerned. And the audience sing it back to us. Luckily we've only the two that everybody knows when it comes to popular songs."

"All Around My Hat" wasn't actually the first single issued from the album of the same name – that was "Hard Times In Old England".

"We thought that was more commercial, if anything," recalls Maddy. "But then the first thing we'd had success with was an unaccompanied Latin chant. How bizarre could it get? So we were kind of up for anything. I wanted to jig about the stage and have a good time. We were sort of completely cut loose, really."

Maddy rejects the suggestion that Batt's introduction to the Steeleye Span fold was a premeditated move to broaden their appeal. "We kind of always ploughed our own furrow. We'd always had some popularity. We were selling out gigs here at that point, so we were kind of successful in English terms, but not in the pop world. But then we never expected to be in the pop world. That wasn't what we were trying for. He wasn't particularly brought in to make us more commercial. We just wanted it to be different, that's how I remember it.

"Success was not something we didn't want, but I don't think we were trying to be in the pop world like other people. We were trying to do what we did and make it popular. There was a slightly different emphasis. We were looking to change what we did in order to be popular. We tried a couple of things after that, after the success, but then we sort of gave up on that because we realised it wasn't what we were good at.

"We never stopped touring and recording. We had a deal with Chrysalis for ten albums in five years. We didn't manage that, but we did do quite a lot. We did become somewhat cavalier with the recording process, is the way to describe it!

"People didn't recognise me elsewhere. The odd time people did, which rather irritated me, actually. I wasn't a person who wants to be known outside my work. And I hated people photographing me if I was out. We weren't that huge. In those days we weren't on the television all the time, and there weren't videos out. It was just hysterical. We laughed all the time. And then we fought! I wouldn't have missed it. It was a very funny band to be in. Very passionate. We literally fought, physically, chucking beer over each other and stuff like that. We were very involved in what we were doing. We took the music very seriously but I don't know that we took ourselves that seriously. I like to think we didn't!"

Batt's association with Steeleye Span came to an end after *Rocket Cottage* – described by Rob Young as "the sound of a group forgetting its reason for being"[64] – whose bombast was completely out of kilter with the explosion of punk in 1976. The sessions for the album took place in the town of Hilversum in the Netherlands, and afforded Batt the opportunity to exercise his inner Brian Eno.

"We lived in a little hotel on the edge of town and we used to ride into the studio on bikes," Batt remembers. "It was the summer of '76 and it was very hot. I remember wearing nothing but a pair of shorts. With 'Fighting For Strangers', I thought, 'Let's make a really weird record here'. We put the rhythm down first, all sorts of percussion toys like shakers, finger cymbals and bongos. We put together this clanking sound like an army marching along. I turned the lights out and made it all sort of arty farty. We got Maddy to sing the song over it, without any accompaniment at all. And we went off to the pub.

"When we came back, we picked another key and she sang it all through again, starting in a different place. So we had one of her starting in one key at one place, and one of her starting in another key at another place. But we didn't know which was which, because we weren't listening to the first one when we did the second one. When it came to mixing it, we had all this weird percussion going on. We were moving it from left to right. I was doing an impression of Brian Eno, really! Then I brought the vocals up, both of them, in different keys and faded them in and out against each other. It worked really well."

Shortly after the release of the album, which was poorly promoted by Chrysalis, Batt and Steeleye Span went their separate ways. It was all very amicable. "I look back on it with a great deal of affection," he says. "It was a really nice time with great people. There wasn't one person in the band who I didn't get on with. There were people within the band who didn't necessarily get on with each other from time to time. Peter Knight would have the occasional tiff with Tim, and I occasionally had to step in as referee."

❡

Few were surprised when Knight subsequently quit the band along with Bob Johnson, both feeling aggrieved that Chrysalis had allegedly duped them into working on *Rocket Cottage* with the promise of recording their project, *The King Of Elfland's Daughter*.

Elf City

Once more Steeleye Span were imploding. The writing had been on the wall for some time if anyone had bothered to pay attention. Conceptually there was a transition from the sublime to the ridiculous – or, as Martin Carthy succinctly puts it, "Steeleye was elf city" – and episodes of high farce. These included the addition of an extra member, Mr Steeleye, an actor decked out in mask, cloak and thigh-length silver boots, who, at an open air concert in Crystal Palace, danced with Maddy before boarding a small boat to row across the lake and dance with the faithful. At least that was the plan. Halfway across, the hapless Mr Steeleye found himself set upon by over enthusiastic fans splashing about in the water. As the boat tipped over, Mr Steeleye, suddenly remembering that he couldn't swim, pleaded for rescue.

Then there was the concert at London's Hammersmith Odeon indicative of the kind of excesses in the 1970s that provoked the punk rebellion. Steeleye Span's set climaxed with their fee for the show, £8,500, raining down on the audience from holes that had been drilled in the roof – a stunt devised by manager Tony Secunda, also Svengali to The Moody Blues, Procol Harum, The Move and T-Rex.

"Tony said the publicity it made couldn't have been bought for that," says Maddy.

"I remember standing there when this money was raining down, and of course we might as well not have been there. It sort of takes away from the band. But that was Tony Secunda. Again, I wouldn't have missed him. He was a pain in the arse, he was difficult, tricky, all the rest of it, and he'd land you in all kinds of trouble, but again, it's not something you'd want to miss."

Following his death in 1995, Secunda was described in an obituary by Chris Welch as:

a dark, brooding and somewhat menacing figure, [who] thrived on taking risks, and he was not afraid to indulge in the most basic scams and publicity stunts. But he achieved results for his artists and took the ethics of the underground hippie scene into the boardrooms of the music industry.[65]

Martin Carthy is less magnanimous, alluding to "the late and un-lamented" Secunda as "a nasty man, dreadful man."

It was Carthy to whom Steeleye Span turned following the exit of Knight and Johnson – and, with an irony not lost on anyone, free reed instrumentalist John Kirkpatrick.

"Maddy rang me up and told me what she was thinking," says Carthy. "Pete and Bob had just done a concept album dedicated to a Lord Dunsany story (*The King Of Elfland's Daughter*). It rather dumped the rest of the band. They had a tour of Australia and the States lined up, neither of which came off. Maddy had decided it was time for the band to finish. She'd made a solo album and had decided she wanted to give that her best attention. But there was some business to clear up. She asked me in order to bring the whole thing back full circle, and to ask John Kirkpatrick. I laughed and said, 'What a great idea!'"

This line-up released *Storm Force Ten* and *Live At Last!* before the group was finally dissolved.

"I think we were just completely worn out," says Maddy. "We just didn't stop. And I think that the tensions in the band had become overpowering. With all the recording, we hardly had time to do what we were good at. We were sort of run into the ground. And actually, we should have just taken time out, which a band now would do – you would take a year or two out. But you couldn't do that then. It was like, 'No, you can't – it'll all be gone. The people won't come back'. But of course that's rubbish. That was coming from Tony and the record company – probably more Tony. So we decided to split.

"Pete and Bob had already gone, so we brought in Martin and John. That was lovely, actually, but they had other things to do and didn't want to be in a band for any length of time, so they just came in to finish off the work we'd got in the book, as it were. We could have just said, 'We're not doing it. We're going to take time out for a year, eighteen months, or however long it takes'."

Eight

Pictures In My Head

♪

June Tabor was an Oxford undergraduate when she first met Maddy Prior. The university folk club would occasionally host touring acts, and, on this particular occasion, Maddy and Tim Hart were booked to play. "We hit it off straight away," says June.

"She was doing a floor spot in a club," Maddy remembers. "We got to know her and went to have dinner at hers a few times – certainly I did. Everybody knew everybody round the folk scene, all the performers. We were of the same age and of the same mind. We liked the same stuff. We liked the same players, although we had very different ways of doing it."

Subsequently their paths crossed at various festivals up and down the country. June moved to London and found a flat in trendy Muswell Hill, a bus ride away from Maddy's place in Archway. They became fast friends. Maddy was – and remains – "a kindred". It was only a matter of time, and timing, before a working relationship developed. The Silly Sisters project was essentially conceived at Bromyard Festival in 1973.

June recalls, "We were sitting in the back row – there was a whole line of us, all good singers, singing harmonies with whatever was happening on stage. Royston Wood was one, and Clive Woolf, and a chap from Wales called Jim Harper, and Maddy and me. And we were sitting next to each other singing, and just sort of looked at each other and said, 'That sort of sounded good, didn't it? Come on, let's work something out together'."

Maddy's version substantiates June's, with the addition of one minor detail – they were slightly inebriated.

The first song they tried out together was "Four Loom Weaver", a 19th Century lament probably derived from "The Poor Cotton Weaver" (written after the Napoleonic Wars) and revived by Ewan MacColl in 1951. A mutual fondness for Bulgarian-style harmonies informed their version. Bulgarian vocal music, uniquely, "is dominated by women singers with athletic voices, and includes a wide range of vocal gymnastics such as whoops, yips and trills. It also makes use of a huge dynamic range, from a near whisper to a loud, piercing style often referred to as 'open throated' by western listeners, although ironically it involves an extreme tightening of the throat."[66]

June and Maddy actually arranged a couple of songs in Bulgarian and hatched a mischievous ruse to premiere them before an unsuspecting public.

Says June: "We had planned to hire some Bulgarian traditional costumes, with false wigs, and then we'd get someone at a festival where the stage was distant – Cleethorpes, somewhere like that – to say, 'Now we have a surprise delegation from Bulgaria', and go on in Bulgarian dress, sing two songs in Bulgarian and not speak, see if anyone knew who we were. But we never did it! We never got round to it. I can still remember the words of one of them, which is no mean feat."

It wasn't just the harmonious coalescence of their voices that made them such an accomplished duo, but a reciprocity in technique.

"We discovered that we phrased in the same way when we're singing together. I find it quite difficult to sing with another person, but with Maddy we kind of breathe in the same places and phrase a song in the same way when singing with each other. That was half the battle of actually doing it. We do still do it occasionally. The problem is that my voice has gone down and Maddy's has gone up, and I don't sing harmonies anymore. So, although I can remember mostly what I did then, I can't work out new stuff now. We used to switch. That was one of the things about when we were singing together. Whoever was singing the tune and whoever was singing the harmony would switch over halfway, or at a certain point, and then it would cross back again. That's what makes it so individual, I suppose, those recordings on that first album. It just happened that way – it just was. It just worked."

That first album was *Silly Sisters*, released by Chrysalis Records in 1976, a collection of songs about work, religion and conjugal relations, soaked in humour, tragedy and absurdism. Songs such as "Doffin' Mistress", first recorded by Anne Briggs in 1963, "Burning Of Auchindoon" (on which Maddy does a convincing Scottish accent), a Child ballad concerning a 1592 feud between the Huntly family and the Earl of Moray, Cyril Tawney's "The Grey Funnel Line", a description of the daily life of a sailor in the Royal Navy, and "Silver Whistle", a Jacobite composition translated from Gaelic, followed by a Johnny Moynihan tune.

"It came together organically," says June. "We'd get together occasionally and work on something else after doing 'Four Loom Weaver'. Maddy would show up when I was doing a solo gig at somewhere like the Florence in Islington, and she'd just get up and do two or three songs with me as part of my gig. We'd acquired a small repertoire after a couple of years. Then she got the opportunity to do a project album after Steeleye had had a Top 10 hit with 'All Around My Hat'. She said she wanted to do an album with me.

"We'd got quite a lot of the songs worked out or semi worked out, because we'd been doing it for fun for a bit, and done floor spots in clubs. We came up with a list of songs and she said, 'Well, we're going to have to have people on it. Who do we want?' And pretty much everybody we asked said they'd do it. Then you have the whole process of sitting down and rehearsing things. They had to fit in with the way that we had worked the songs out to a degree. When you're singing with somebody else, it becomes more regular as to how you do something."

According to Maddy, Chrysalis wanted her to work on a project separate from Steeleye Span. "I probably came up with the idea of doing something with June, using the traditional people, the revival people that we knew. Like Nic (Jones), Martin (Carthy), and Andy (Irvine) and Johnny (Moynihan), who I'm a great fan of. It was so nice to go into a proper studio with an engineer who had a different sensibility sound-wise. The folk albums are lovely, and I have a lot of them, but they have a different sensibility sound-wise. It was probably the first album of traditional material that was done on 24-track. We went into Morgan Studios, which was a pop studio, and that's not where the folk world was. We multi-tracked and did it like people do in 24-track studios. The folk world, as I recollect it – I may be wrong here – was basically recording live, and not with many people, generally speaking. There wasn't a lot of tracking. I felt that going into Morgan Studios was something different, with Robin Black, who was a brilliant engineer."

The impressive cast of musicians on the album not only featured Jones, Carthy, Irvine and Moynihan, but the grandmaster of the double bass, Danny Thompson. According to John Tobler, *Silly Sisters* "attracted considerable attention among folk fans, especially devotees of Maddy's talents, who were pleased to hear her singing again in the style which had first brought her to prominence, as opposed to the more rock-oriented direction which Steeleye Span had adopted".[67]

There was no promotional tour – Chrysalis weren't keen, June claimed to J.P. Bean:

"They didn't actually want Maddy to do the album, so we played in some rather strange places which weren't commensurate with the fuss that had been made. There were a couple of discos. There was one like an Alpine village – it was in Liverpool or Newcastle."[68]

§

June's collaboration with Maddy had not only increased her profile and established her reputation beyond the parameters of the folk sphere – by dint of Maddy's mainstream renown – it also elicited interest from Steeleye Span's manager, Tony Secunda. June was wary of becoming the latest recruit to his roster. She wanted autonomy over her artistic direction. And besides, she was still a working girl. "If he was the typical music manager, I thought I wouldn't have much control over what I was doing. I was kind of determined to maintain control over what I sang and how I sang it, because I didn't want to fall out of love with it, in a way – to not be able to do it the way that I wanted to do it. The way to do that was not to become a full-time musician, but to work in the library and do very modest gigs in a kind of semi-professional second career. I did that certainly the whole time I worked in the library.

"That's one thing about working in a library. Library hours are long, but you don't have to work all of them. So you get a day and half off one week and two days off another week, because the week runs Monday to Saturday. You'd work late some nights but not others. The chap who did the timesheets was very sympathetic. So it was possible to have two careers. I was doing about fifteen gigs a month quite often. Trains used to run back late at night. They don't do that anymore. The *Silly Sisters* album was recorded in my annual holiday one year, and then we did some gigs in my annual holiday the next year!"

There was a second Silly Sisters album in 1988. Again, *No More To The Dance* featured some crack musicians, including Huw Warren and Mark Emerson, both of whom would become June's regular accompanists, and Breton guitarist Dan Ar Braz, once briefly of Fairport Convention, who recorded eight albums with harpist Alan Stivell between 1972 and 1977.

"Dan's a lovely guitarist who's great on ideas about music," Maddy told Simon Jones.

"He's worked so long in Celtic styles with Stivell that he's learned many approaches to music that not many musicians are familiar with. The man's a master of free time playing. What the Silly Sisters do is largely Celtic, so he fits in easily. I can relate to the swings and rhythms in his playing, so there is a crossover point between him and me. He understands both sides. June is more used to free singing and an introspective approach, where I'm more extrovert in the way I do things. But that works well together."[69]

No More To The Dance is certainly more instrumentally expansive than its predecessor, with Ar Braz's picking particularly prominent throughout, but once again it's all about the voices – fervent, euphonious and almost telepathic in their compatibility across material from the traditional "Cakes And Ale" and "Hedger And Ditcher", to the contemporary "Blood And Gold", written by Andy Irvine, and Colum Sands' "Almost Every Circumstance".

There hasn't been another Silly Sisters album since, although Maddy and June have appeared together on stage many times, including a spellbinding performance of "Four Loom Weaver" at the BBC's Electric Proms in 2008.

"I'd love to do another album," says Maddy. "We've sort of talked about it. The difficulty is getting material to suit us. I think there is a body of work – I'm a great believer in threes. It's funny about working on a project – there's something that needs to fire up. We met up a couple of times and it didn't. And sometimes there's no reason why. I think it would be worth having another go, but I think we'd probably need to work with other musicians to get us to move somewhere with it."

June attributes the failure to launch a third collection to the fact she no longer sings harmony. "When we did the first album, I used to go to folk clubs and sing around, all that kind of thing. Although I don't have any genuine musical knowledge, I could sing harmonies in a way. And also, my voice was quite a bit higher. It's very hard now to do things whereby the voices can cross over, which they did on the first album. They didn't really on the second one. The harmonies had to be more rigid. On the first album, sometimes I'd sing the tune and I'd sing the harmonies in the same verse just by swapping over, and that's why the voices work so well together. But we can't do that anymore. It's just genuinely hard to find a way to make it work. And if it doesn't work, there's no point in artificially creating it."

♪

June may have rebuffed Tony Secunda's management approach, but when Topic Records came calling she couldn't refuse. The label had, several years previously, already asked her to do a solo album.

"I couldn't decide what to put on the proposed album and things just went on and on. And then we started thinking about doing the Silly Sisters one with Maddy, so the idea got left for a bit,"[70] she told Fred Dellar.

"Finally, two people helped me put it together. One was Isobel Sutherland, who said, 'Come on, you've got to do a record – now here's a pen and here's a piece of paper. Just write down what you're going to do on it'.

"And the other was Paul Brown (co-manager of Decameron and Cajun Moon), who helped me get things together and offered a lot of constructive criticism. I've known Paul since I was at Oxford – we were friends at college. He's actually a metallurgist, but now he's got this management thing going with Sandy Robertson. He's been my mentor, so to speak."

Unused as June was to the recording process (the *Silly Sisters* album was the first time she had recorded in a proper studio), *Airs And Graces*, her solo debut, is sparsely instrumented, with Jon Gillaspie on piano, organ, roxichord, bassoon and sopranino, Tony Hall on melodeon and Nic Jones on acoustic guitar and fiddle.

"I thought I'd quite like to have some accompaniment on it, having gone through this learning process of working with very good accompanists on the *Silly Sisters*. So, Nic and I did a few gigs together, in as much as I sang some songs unaccompanied and he accompanied me on some songs. But the version of 'When Gamekeepers Lie Sleeping' we did on the album, he actually put an accompaniment on it. And how the hell he did, I don't know! I did it first and then he accompanied it afterwards. It's the way a lot of gypsy singers sing. They change the time signature and pause here. I think it's a fantastic way of singing – that's what I was trying to do with that song. Nic managed to put an accompaniment to it. I don't think we would ever have managed to have done it live.

"The way that an album is put together – and this is not something I do since – would be to do a guide vocal, then to put all the other instruments on and then re-do the vocals. So I suppose I was kind of infected by that slightly on *Airs And Graces*. But I've since discovered that that is not the way I can make an album. I find you get the best performance if it's the real vocal with the real instrument. It was an eye opener to discover that things were done in bits and then put together."

June's choice of songs is impeccable, indicative of a discerning taste she has consistently displayed in the four decades since. "Bonny May", the first of three Child Ballads, this one culled from several texts, was anglicised "with the aid and inspiration of Maddy".[71] There's recognition of Belle Stewart's influence on a reverent reading of "Queen Among The Heather", and an inspired "Plains Of Waterloo". But the track that makes you still your breath for all of its six minutes and nineteen seconds is June's *a cappella* rendition of Eric Bogle's "The Band Played Waltzing Matilda". This young Australian soldier's account of the Battle of Gallipoli during the First World War – conveyed in the blunt language of realism – dispels the myth of cause in any conflict, instead emphasising its legacy of human carnage, the obscenity of so much death within a context blithely referred to by present day hawks as a theatre. Bogle allows no room for ambiguity. War is futile. It is barbaric. And even those who survive the ordeal are changed forever.

Bogle, who emigrated from Scotland to Australia in 1969, chose songwriting "to become popular at parties, to help seduce women, to become rich and famous – and maybe to help me understand the world I lived in and the people I shared it with". He wrote "The Band Played Waltzing Matilda" two years later, having witnessed his first Anzac Day march in Canberra [Anzac Day is an annual commemoration of the war dead in Australia and New Zealand].

"In 1971, the Vietnam War was still going, and Australian soldiers were still dying there," he says. "As I was part of the Moratorium movement that opposed the war, I thought that the time was right for an anti-war song. However, in spite of the fact that Aussie boys were dying across there, few Australians could actually point to where Vietnam was on a map of the world, and by this time reports about the war were relegated to page six in most newspapers.

"I decided to set the song in Gallipoli, as the stories, myths and legends regarding that campaign are deeply entrenched in the Australian national consciousness – every Australian school kid knows them. And it really doesn't matter about which war you are actually referring to, because the end results of all wars are pretty much the same – death, destruction, loss, grief and so on."

The song took Bogle three weeks to write. The original draft was eight verses and between ten and fifteen minutes long, "depending on how drunk I was when I sang it. After my audiences started committing mass hari-kari after the sixth verse, I recognised I had to rewrite it, if only to save some innocent lives! I wanted to reduce it to four verses but couldn't manage it. I could only edit it down to five verses, and that's the structure it maintains to this day."

Bogle discounts the suggestion that "The Band Played Waltzing Matilda" has acquired a kind of immortality. "The song may outlast me by a few years, but will not last forever. Nothing does. Maybe one day in the far distant future, when the war is a fading ghost from a dim, half-remembered past, the song will be finally consigned to the dustbin of history, where it ultimately belongs."

There are many among us who would beg to differ with Bogle's prognosis. But let's return to June's rendering. Her delivery of the lyric is freighted with the requisite measure of cynical enlightenment. She offers a stoic, imperturbable characterisation of the soldier, yet it's none the less heartbreaking for that. June's relationship with "The Band Played Waltzing Matilda" began in 1974.

"Throughout the whole time I've been singing, there have been occasions when songs have found me. And it was almost supposed to happen. That was the first. I was staying with some friends in Wiltshire, who had lived in Australia for a while. They had two other people staying, one Australian and one a Channel Islander who they had known when they lived in Australia. We all went to a sing around in the back room of a pub near Bath, called the Pack Horse.

And Lorraine, who was the Australian, said to Jane (Herivel), 'Go on, sing it'. And she said, 'Are you sure?' And Lorraine said, 'Yeah!' And Jane stood up and sang, 'The Band Played Waltzing Matilda'. She knew Eric Bogle. I sat there and the tears poured down my face, and I thought, 'I want to sing that song'. I asked her if she would give me the song and she said she'd love to, but she had to ask Eric first. So, I learnt it but I didn't sing it anywhere until I heard back and Eric said it was OK.

"I started singing it at gigs. I remember doing it at Inverness Festival, which was in a big ballroom in the Caledonian Hotel, one of those conveyor belt concerts when you can do three or four songs. I forget what the first one I did was. The second one was the First World War song, 'Hanging On The Old Barbed Wire'. Then I did 'Waltzing Matilda', and people still talk about how that was the first time they'd heard it. There's a lovely line in Sebastian Barry's novel *A Long Long Way* where somebody stands up and sings a song, and the men are all listening – again it's the First World War. And when he finishes there is silence. And then the book says, 'It was the silence after the song that pleased the singer most'. And it was just like that. There was this total silence after I'd sung the last line, and then people started clapping, though they were going, 'Oh, my God'.

"I'd been interested by the First World War from when I was quite young. But that was the beginning of singing about it."

There have been many versions of the song – Joan Baez, Liam Clancy, The Dubliners, The Pogues, Christy Moore and even novelist Garrison Keillor are among those who have covered it. But "The Band Played Waltzing Matilda", because of her definitive interpretation, will always be inextricably linked with June. Don't take my word for it – just ask its composer.

"I love every version," claims Bogle. "It's the ultimate compliment a songwriter can be paid, when someone likes your song well enough to sing it or record it. If pushed though, I'd have to nominate June's as one of my favourite versions, along with one by Alex Campbell. It's her voice, her phrasing, her innate sense of vocal drama and emphasis – the whole damn thing, in fact. It's one of the few unaccompanied versions of the song, and one of the even fewer interpretations by a female."

June imparts a rib-tickling anecdote concerning Liam Clancy's adaptation, which features on the 1976 album, *Tommy Makem And Liam Clancy*, a huge seller in his native Ireland.

"Archie Fisher recorded it, if I remember, and gave it to Liam. I met Liam many years later and he said, 'Oh yeah, Archie gave it to me – that built me a house, you know!'"

June may not have shifted the kind of units that Makem and Clancy did with "The Band Played Waltzing Matilda", but she certainly stirred hearts and provoked consciences with a memorable reading of it during a John Peel session for BBC Radio One in 1975.

"I ended up doing the session by default," she says. "Tim and Maddy were supposed to be doing it. Maddy had lost her voice. Tim rang me up and said, 'I don't want to lose this session, but I can't do it on my own – I don't know enough songs. Will you come along and I'll do two or three songs, and you can do two or three songs, and then we won't lose the session?' So I went down to the BBC with him. I met John Walters, who was John Peel's producer. My only experience of working at the BBC until then was, 'Keep it short and bright, no longer than three minutes'.

"So I said, 'There's a song I'd really like to sing but it's quite long'. And he said, 'Oh, yeah? How long is it?' 'Six minutes'. He said, 'Well, the longest thing we've had on so far was Tangerine Dream, and that was about seventeen minutes, so I think we can get away with six!' Peeley was the exception in terms of letting people do what they wanted to do – and John Walters. So I sang 'Waltzing Matilda' on that session. And again, people still come up to me and say, 'I remember hearing you sing that'. People say, 'I was at boarding school and I wasn't supposed to be listening to the radio, but I got a little transistor and listened to it under the bedclothes. And I've never forgotten hearing you sing that song'.

"I still sing it now and again. I stopped singing it for a while because it had become known and people started joining in with it. It's not a chorus song. Fine if that's what they wanted to do, but for me that wasn't the way it should go."

This is a position with which Bogle concurs, quipping, "It's hardly 'Roll Out The Barrel', is it?!" Whenever he performs the song, however, "there's a sort of low level hum from the audience, as many of them can't help singing along very softly".

Fittingly, June performed "The Band Played Waltzing Matilda" – with accompanists Huw Warren and Mark Emerson – at the official opening of the In Flanders Fields Museum in Ypres, "the greatest anti-war museum I have ever seen". Turns out the inauguration was on Anzac Day.

"We did 'Will Ye Go To Flanders' and something else, and then I sang 'The Band Played Waltzing Matilda' to a very large audience of dignitaries. Robin Cook was there, but I never got to meet him, sadly. Again, the silence after the song was incredible. And then people started clapping. Huw said afterwards, 'I'm glad you couldn't see behind me when you were singing, because there was just silent black and white footage of Gallipoli'.

"I have sung it again since, just occasionally. Because I knew I had to sing it then, and I hadn't sung it for a long time, I took the dogs up into the woods and thought, 'I'll just walk through the woods and go through the words in my head'. I only got to verse three and I was crying so hard, the dogs are looking at me, sort of going, 'What's the matter, Mum? You alright?' But when it came to do it for real, the song carried me through and I didn't break down. But it's such an incredibly visual song. All the best songs to me are pictures in my head – like having a cinema in my head – and that's one of them. I can see each scene as it unfolds. It's quite extraordinary."

With 2014 marking the centenary of the outbreak of the First World War, "The Band Played Waltzing Matilda'" is particularly poignant at this time. However, with the almost constant state of combat in the world, the song always seems to be relevant. Bogle is well aware of this fact, "I suppose the song remains relevant as the human race still embroils itself in various nasty, bloody little conflicts now and then. Sad, really".

Nine

Stepping Out Of The Shadows

♪

Steeleye Span are not so much a band as an institution. Personnel come and go – some go and come back again – but the ethos remains constant. How to describe that ethos? Offering a wholly subjective, and possibly simplistic interpretation, I would suggest it's about both paying deference to traditional English music while simultaneously finding ways to reinvent that music. The business of reinvention is, no less than the business of invention itself, a precarious one.

Concepts invariably appear exciting at the moment of their conception, yet some concepts, in being realised, reveal nothing more than their superficiality, best consigned to the realm of the ephemeral, attributable to a momentary lapse of aesthetic instinct. They fail, in other words.

Still, there is something laudable – meritorious, even – in those creatively bold enough to risk the derision of an audience, whether that's an audience of advocates or critics. Steeleye Span have always possessed this boldness, and have consequently sounded rather foolish on occasion. Especially in the 1980s when, as Maddy acknowledges, they had "gone in slightly different directions. It was much harder for us to make the music meld in the same way."

The split that followed *Storm Force Ten* and *Live At Last!* didn't endure. And so they reformed, with Rick Kemp and Bob Johnson returning to the fold. By now, Steeleye Span had functioned as a group for more than a decade, and had, with the departure of Terry and Gay Woods following *Hark! The Village Wait* in 1970, established what became a recurring theme of ever-changing line-ups.

Maddy attempts to rationalise Steeleye's longevity, why she won't – or can't – let it lie: "One of the things about being in a band is you never, ever get that same thing in any other circumstance, musically. That band is that band. And it's the only musical experience you have of that band. There's a stability in that band that I don't have in other circumstances in the same way. There's a freedom within that band, because it's so established in my own head, and in my body almost. They are the group that they are. That's what works. Not the music being better – it's by its flaws it's almost known, in a funny kind of way.

"It's not as straightforward as everyone being good players, otherwise it would be easier to put bands together that worked. It's indefinable. Each band has its own credo and attitude about what it does that's almost, again, indefinable. There is a kind of system with each band, and that applies to the different line-ups as well. They have a different rationale as to why they're doing what they're doing and why they're doing it."

In 1980, they did it because Chrysalis approached them to do it. "They asked us to make an album. We got together and thought we'd go on the road with it, now we're here!" said Maddy pragmatically.

The album was *Sails Of Silver*, which Maddy recorded when pregnant with her first child. Produced by Gus Dudgeon, renowned for his association with Elton John, his input was "greater than any previous producer and this gives a more accessible album in many ways".[72]

But as Maddy told John Tobler, "the band didn't settle so easily".[73] Within two years, Tim Hart had quit. It was the end of a musical relationship with Maddy that had spanned three decades, two albums as a duo and every incarnation of Steeleye Span. Speaking in 1994 Tim explained that:

> I left for really personal reasons. One, I wanted to spend more time with the wife and kids. Secondly, I'd done a couple of kids' albums, nursery rhyme albums, during that intervening period, and I enjoyed

working with Andy Richards, the synthesiser player, and I found I had much more freedom for my ideas working with Andy, and I kind of got fed up with the thought of having to go back to Steeleye. This tour came up and I made my mind up. I thought, "I don't want this anymore".[74]

There were another pair of albums, *Back In Line* (1982) and *Tempted And Tried* (1989), and further departures, including Rick Kemp, then Maddy's husband.

"During the '80s, our lives were full of distractions and confusions," she says. "Peter (Knight) spent time on his instrument and became involved in improvisation and matured considerably in his playing. But it was a long road. Bob (Johnson) became involved in opening a restaurant and went to university and obtained a degree in psychology. Nigel (Pegrum, drummer) had run a studio, Rick and I toured with our own band, recorded four albums and were raising a family."[75]

Steeleye Span staggered on, replacing Kemp with Tim Harries, and Pegrum with Liam Genockey, but a defining sound eluded this latest version. "We struggled with it. It's always been a bit of a curate's egg," admits Maddy. "When you're trying different things, some of it is going to work and some of it isn't. When they say that it's a risk, the risk is that you'll fail. It's not that the risk is negligible and you'll be successful. Some of it doesn't work. We did do a reggae-spotted cow at one point. We decided that wasn't a good idea. Then Edward II came along and did everything reggae, which was very weird.

"We did try everything. We wanted things to be different. There were no rules. Once you weren't going to do the folk things, there were no rules. Once you went to America, that changed everything because you were suddenly out of that folk bubble. It had tended to be very narrow. I did do some work in folk clubs at the time with June after that."

The folk clubs welcomed her as though she'd never been away. And indeed as far as Maddy's concerned, she never was. Whether with Tim, as part of Steeleye or in her solo career, she has always drawn from this source.

"I still do traditional music," she says. "I don't necessarily do it in the way that the revival has decided it should be done. But I still do a lot of traditional music. Sometimes it's just the words that are traditional and we've put other tunes to it. But, in my head, this whole thing comes from the traditional. And the good thing about traditional music is that it doesn't have that youth quality!"

Meanwhile, the bastard progeny of the traditional and the contemporary – electric folk, or folk rock, if you prefer – as represented by Steeleye Span was in its death throes. Some would say *rigor mortis* had already set in. Dr Britta Sweers, in *Electric Folk: The Changing Face Of English Traditional Music*, cited the emergence of punk, new wave, disco and funk as the reasons for its demise by the end of the 1970s. Punk, in particular, "seemed to exert an especially strong influence upon the process, leading also in a completely different direction: while the old electric folk groups seemed to have disappeared, one could observe a modified folk rock direction coming into being."[76]

This modified direction involved almost a complete refutation of traditional material and traditional songwriting templates, both of which Steeleye Span and their ilk had incorporated, in favour of politically-charged songs about the state of the nation.

Dr Sweers has now slightly revised her theory about punk being principally to blame for electric folk's dwindling popularity: "It is very easy to blame changing music interests in the mid-1970s alone. There seem to have been a mixture of issues. Some bands, like Fairport Convention, had been struggling with constant member changes, which also affected the style. There seem to have been power issues in other bands. Pentangle disbanded in 1972, also due to the touring stress – whether folk or electric folk, the number of gigs is extremely high.

"It sometimes seems that the bands were also somehow stuck on a musical level – the various styles of electric folk were fusion forms. Regarding folk rock, rock kept changing, yet folk rock bands

JUNE

Two shots of a young June, taken in Autumn 1966 and sometime in 1967. (*Unknown photographers. Images courtesy of June Tabor*)

June with Oyster Band in 1991.
(*Images by Genia Ainsworth. Courtesy of June Tabor*)

Top: Lovely reflective picture of June, circa 2005.
(*Image by John Haxby. Courtesy of June Tabor*)

Above: June with long time collaborator Martin Simpson, for Martin
Simpson & Friends set, Sidmouth 2012. (*Image by Candy Schwartz*)

June at Sidmouth 2012.
(*Images by Judith Burrrows. Courtesy of June Tabor*)

kept attached to their old styles and partly also the sound that had emerged in the late 1960s."

Mike Brocken isn't convinced that electric folk did actually die, though he does concede that "for some in the late '70s, punk was more authentic than either folk or folk rock, which could be viewed as self-indulgent. Synthesisers dropped in price, making it very cheap to make any music. Ageing folkies would not really hand the baton over to a younger generation in the late '70s – in fact, they tended to retreat back into their manuscripts. Left wing politics were becoming pragmatically very problematic. I suppose one might also argue that, musically, folk rock in the '70s became something of a musical cul-de-sac. The Pogues, The Oyster Band and The Levellers did much to keep a folk rock aesthetic going, and their albums still sound interesting up to a point. But there is a lot of generic repetition in recent years."

This isn't a debate Maddy cares for, just as it wasn't a debate she cared for back in the day: "These categories are a load of old rubbish. There's no way that Fairport and us are at all alike, or Pentangle. Yet we're all lumped in together. Our attitudes and our way of doing things are very different. We don't think of ourselves as the same. Nobody wants to be in a particular bag. The truth is every band is different. Every band did it differently and came from different places. Most of us have had a go at doing a bit of rock music."

¶

Away from Steeleye Span, and two years after the first *Silly Sisters* album with June Tabor, Maddy finally made her bow as a solo artist. *Woman In The Wings* was co-produced by old friend Ian Anderson, and featured Jethro Tull in their entirety. He didn't hesitate when asked by Maddy to help out.

"I liked her and respected her, and I wasn't washing my hair that week – at a time when I actually had some!" he jokes. "She had some great basic song ideas and the lyrics. So we recorded backing tracks with the Tull guys, and then my engineer, Robin Black, David

Palmer and I tried to put it all together. It was a team effort. Pan's People's Cherry Gillespie and my wife, Shona, sang backing vocals on one track ('Catseyes').

"I seem to remember Maddy's vocal quality was quite difficult to record as she had such a pure mid-range timbre, and pushed the limits of recording technology getting it on to tape in a way to do justice to that wonderful cutting and articulate vocal quality. When she felt she wasn't up to doing her best, she would call in and say she wouldn't be in that day. So we could concentrate instead on getting backing tracks done and preparing for the next session. She knew what she could do and what standards she had to achieve. So I went for an early curry and waited for her to call again!"

According to Anderson, Maddy knew exactly what she was looking for on the album and "had plenty of input. She wasn't afraid to say something if she didn't like my ideas or efforts. The title speaks for itself. Maddy stepping out of the shadows of the band identity, in her mind at least. Of course, to the rest of us, she was the focal point of the band."

He considered it quite brave "to stand aside from the band success and risk all in doing a solo (album). And a chance to make a more autobiographical statement. Heart on the sleeve sort of stuff. She created a feeling of personal vulnerability in her songs. A big change from the rather remote incantations of historical lyrics and sentiments often watered down through the decades and centuries of partial decay. That was why it was good to do. Maddy singing from the heart and soul of Maddy, rather than as an academic custodian of British traditional folk. But I could feel she was under pressure and nervous about the outcome."

Nervous or not, Maddy was sufficiently buoyed by the project to seek out other ventures, to establish a separate persona from Steeleye Span. By the end of 1978, she had guested on Mike Oldfield's *Incantations*, and the following year made an appearance on his *Exposed* set.

Another solo album – *Changing Winds* – followed the same year. There were just a couple in the 1980s (*Hooked On Winning* and

Going For Glory) and a handful in the 1990s. The noughties were Maddy's most prolific period, with the concept albums, *Arthur The King* and *Lionhearts*, affirming her status as an artist of considerable substance in her own right.

"I've always had this kind of thing that one song is very short. I like bigger ideas and flows," she says. "And so, things like 'Wee Weaver' (on Steeleye Span's *Ten Man Mop, Or Mr Reservoir Butler Rides Again*), where I found other sets of words that went round the main song that gave it a little bit more distance and different aspects – that was probably one of the first I did. Then a guy at the wildlife unit in Bristol asked me to write some music for a programme on hares, and I did that ('The Fabled Hare' song cycle on 1993's *Year*). I still think that's actually one of my favourite pieces. That caught a certain atmosphere, I think.

"I like doing the bigger thing, and I like on stage having a swing of songs. When I do a gig I always try to make some movement in it that makes some sort of sense and links in some way. There's a thought process in it. It's not just a load of songs flung out. It doesn't always work with Steeleye because we've got such a variety of material and we've got different lead singers."

The concepts aren't restricted to sound – Maddy likes to incorporate visual imagery where possible: "We did *Ravenchild* with wings. I went to see Steeleye, strangely enough – I was out of the band – and I just thought we had been a very colourful band. I was always dressing up and dancing, and we'd done mummers' plays and all sorts of stuff. And it just looked a bit boring. I thought, 'God, does it look as boring as that?!' I went home that night and I was working on *Ravenchild*. I thought to myself, 'I wonder if I could do wings?'

"I had this stuff in a box, and I had a piece of dowel and it was all absolutely the right dimensions. I couldn't have designed it. It was only later, when I'd worked with it a bit, that I realised how absolutely perfect it was. The wings fell to the floor. If they'd been any longer, they'd have hit the floor. It was just the right length. I made these wings out of black material. On the inside it had silver material, so it looked like feathers. I only used the wings at the end.

I used them in all kinds of different ways. I put them over my head, sang behind them on stage.

"When I first did it in the rehearsal studio, the boys just looked at the floor. I thought, 'If I can do it in front of these two, I can do it in front of anybody!' The thing is, the songs are very vivid for me. I want to get what they're about, across in any way I can, even if it takes more than just singing the song. I use movement quite a lot to describe songs. I want people to get the songs. Of course, the wings completely confused people! Eventually I had to introduce it and tell the audience what was going to happen, because otherwise they hadn't a clue. I loved doing it. I thought it was incredible.

"And then we did the same with *Arthur The King*. Again, I found this piece of material that was perfect. I've no idea what it looked like to the rest of the world! With *Ravenchild*, it got me interested in lighting, because I got them to put a special green light in front of me that shone up, and then put floor lights so when it did the wings, it made an effect. I had a great time! There were some great moments with it. After the first gig that we did, I'd get to the tour van and there'd be a box of Trill on the seat and stuff like that!"

Maddy is not given to displays of narcissism. She's comfortable with her reputation and all that she's done to establish and preserve it, but would rather leave the eulogies to others. Such a reluctance to embrace her legacy is, you suspect, equal parts modesty and insecurity.

"I'm simply not that skilled, basically. I mean, how I got this far being this unskilled amazes me. You need skills in music, really. I think that's why the theatrical side of things – the visual – has worked for me. I'm giving that colour, if you like."

Surely she doesn't believe that occupying a position within the milieu of British music for half a century can be attributed to a propensity for conceptual imagination alone?

"I suppose I've obviously got something, or I wouldn't be here! For me, ideas are so big a part of it, and I'm quite good at that," she admits.

♪

Composer and multi-instrumentalist Troy Donockley was co-producer with Nick Holland on both *Arthur The King* and *Lionhearts*, as well as *Flesh And Blood* (1997), *Ravenchild* (1999) and *Ballads And Candles* (2000). Born in Cumbria, Donockley's parents were part of a band called Travelling Country, and it was through them that he got a fix on folk music.

"Like a lot of budding musicians, I was attracted to its non-mainstream mystique. You felt like you were part of a very musical gang – you had access to a secret hidden from your average pop fan. Same thing with progressive rock," he says.

Steeleye Span, inevitably, formed part of Donockley's learning curve. He was 9 years old when he first heard them on a compilation album his older sister would play. "It had the 'Gaudete' single on it. It blew my mind because it sounded so magical and weird in contrast to The Bay City Rollers and Lieutenant Pigeon. They were arguably the first who made a rock audience aware that folk actually does rock. They were much more adventurous than any other folk rock band at the time. And they looked great too – very hippy and Arcadian.

"The most distinctive thing for me about Maddy was that she sounded wonderfully English and I really related to that. Of course, it goes without saying that she sounded like – and still does – nobody else."

Donockley had encountered Maddy on the live circuit a few times, but finally made her acquaintance properly when they were recording a Status Quo concert at Brixton Academy in 1997.

He recalls how: "We were both performing on their version of 'All Around My Hat', and we hit it off and promised to work together. She then got in touch and we dived in, almost straight to work on the album, *Flesh And Blood*. I was really excited. I loved that voice and wanted to see what would happen. I really had no idea as to if it was going to work, but within hours I knew it would."

For *Flesh And Blood*, and the subsequent albums on which Donockley worked, the songs were "heavily pre-arranged up at Maddy's place. Only when we had the finished map, did we enter the studio."

Rather than punch the clock and record them as rehearsed, the songs continued to develop in the studio.

"Maddy is very open and experimental – absolutely open to suggestion," says Donockley. "Things would just grow. Musically, there was no clear idea, but lyrically, definitely. Three of the albums we did were concept albums, and she forged the words wonderfully. Naturally, this would affect the cadence of the music. Maddy is one of the great British lyricists. And she's a restless musician. All musicians should be that way.

"She is also brilliant at expressing herself into a microphone. She would come up with lots of subtle inflections with different takes. It was always hard choosing. Plus, when we did those albums there was no auto-tune software – like some of her contemporaries, she didn't need it. Those were the days!"

According to Donockley, he and Nick Holland felt consumed by their production duties on Maddy's albums: "I was very composition and arrangement-driven, and he was more experienced with recording and sounds. It was an amazing team."

Donockley's most enjoyable experience, hands down, was *Arthur The King*, a 10-track suite about the legendary British monarch who spearheaded the defence of his country against Saxon invaders in the early sixth century. "It was so ambitious and totally progressive folk, for want of a better description," says Donockley. "Plus, we recorded the whole thing dressed in Arthurian costumes – seriously! – with me as Merlin, Maddy as Guinevere and Nick as Sir Boozalot, sorry, Lancelot! We even dressed our engineer as a court jester."

It was John Dagnell, Maddy's manager and close friend, who proposed a song cycle on King Arthur. "I thought, 'Oh, for fuck's sake, the world's done King Arthur to death. I don't want to do King Arthur'," laughs Maddy. "So I got some books. I read one big tome about Arthur as a Romano British war captain. I thought, 'Oh, that's kind of more interesting'. This was something completely different and I hadn't seen anybody do it that way before."

Donockley and Holland's last collaboration with Maddy was 2003's *Lionhearts*, coincidentally the last original Maddy album (since then, there has been a compilation, *Collections: A Very Best Of 1995 to 2005*, a live set, *The Quest* – recorded at the Theatre Royal, Winchester in 2006, with Donockley on uilleann pipes, electric and acoustic guitars, bouzouki, low and tin whistles and backing vocals – and *Seven For Old England*, featuring songs from the folk music archive).

"On a lot of *Lionhearts*, I would write the words and the three of us would work on the tunes," says Maddy. "I'd say what I thought the music should be, how I thought it should go, and we'd sit there and make it work. Both of them were very good at that."

There are no plans for the threesome to return to the studio in the foreseeable future. According to Donockley: "We are insanely busy with our individual adventures, but I like to think that we will, one day, return to save England in the hour of its most terrible danger. I love the work we did and the extraordinary times we had. She's a one-off. She has that instantly recognisable voice and nobody else could ever sound like her.

— Ten —

Playing Guitar For A Chick

♪

June Tabor comes from the tradition of unaccompanied singing, just like her touchstones, Belle Stewart and Anne Briggs. She has, of course, transcended both in terms of longevity, and arguably in terms of her eminence within the province of British folk music – although it would be an error of critical judgement, and rather too naive, to confine her to this particular genre. For the breadth of June's work – her odyssey of song, if you like – has brought her into territory that has no doubt sent the folk police into apoplexy.

"I don't think of myself as a folk singer. I'm a singer," she says emphatically. "I'm a singer of songs that tell good stories. It doesn't matter where they come from. A lot of it comes from the tradition, but by no means exclusively. And I've gone through phases when I sang very little traditional music. It's come back in again because it's so strong. But to just narrow it down to folk singing is perhaps doing a disservice to all the other kinds of material – though not opera! I haven't got the lungs for opera – that I do continue to sing. It could be a jazz standard, it could be a piece of modern writing. Everybody needs to label things. Otherwise, in the days when there were record shops, where were you going to put it? It has to have some kind of box. It's just that there are quite a few boxes as far as I'm concerned!"

The Guardian newspaper once described her as "quite simply one of Britain's greatest interpreters of popular song... a performer with an extraordinary range and the ability to mix intensity, passion and drama with a chillingly lived in voice that makes every song sound like a personal experience".[77]

Chris Jones, writing on the BBC website in 2003, lauded her as "a paragon of the virtues that folk music holds in its cultural armoury", while noting that her repertoire "has never been blinkered by a quest for authenticity: she has covered all territories from Weimar ballads via jazz to the most trad of trad English folk. And yet, the sense of scholarship she brings to her work never lets you forget that you are listening to, perhaps, the greatest interpreter and curator of indigenous British music." [78]

Elvis Costello went so far as to suggest, "If you don't like listening to June Tabor, you should stop listening to music."[79] Mark that "listening to music" instead of the narrower folk music.

June yielded to her exploratory disposition early on as a recording artist, on the albums that followed *Airs And Graces*, her 1976 debut: *Ashes And Diamonds*, *A Cut Above* – credited jointly with her then accompanist, Martin Simpson – and *Abyssinians*. Alongside traditional songs were contemporary compositions by Dave Goulder ("The Easter Tree"), Richard Thompson ("Strange Affair"), Peter Bond ("Joe Peel"), Andrew Cronshaw ("A Smiling Shore"), Bill Caddick ("Unicorns"), Eric Bogle ("Now I'm Easy") and Joni Mitchell ("The Fiddle And The Drum").

So what criteria does she apply when looking for a song?

"It's always words first," June affirms. "Because usually if the words speak to you in some way, then you can usually – and I say, usually – do something with the tune. It doesn't always work like that, sadly. But a song might make me think, might make me laugh, might make me cry, but most of all, I think, is the strength of visual image. Again, not exclusively, but something that will create that little cinema in my head.

"And the best songs usually – again, not 100% – have economy of language. They don't necessarily tell the entire story. They leave something to your and the listener's imagination. And usually you find these things out afterwards. You go, 'God, that's a great song', and if you bother to find out why it's a great song, or why you want to sing it, then preferably several of these things will come up in your analysis of it, but that's usually afterwards. It's just, 'I've got to sing that'."

June doesn't write songs herself, though she did try once, many years ago. That she ultimately didn't achieve her objective was probably down to the overly ambitious reach of the narrative, which was based on 12th century writer Marie de France.

"It's a werewolf story, and a really strong piece of material," she says. "My aim was to adapt it into English ballad form. But when I got to something like verse 43, I thought, 'Well, no, this isn't really working'. I should have got Gabriel Yacoub to do it, but unfortunately I didn't know him at the time!"[80]

It may seem incongruous that someone as besotted with words and the gradations of language as June, someone who is a voracious reader and indeed whose career, before she committed to singing as a profession, involved being surrounded by books, should choose not to become a writer, in any form, herself. But then again, on reflection, it's a choice that makes perfect sense, given that exposure to and familiarity with literary excellence, whether fiction, poetry or song – which, at its best, does have literary merit – can only lead to the conclusion that everything is merely a repetitive variation on several themes. Put another way, it's all been said before and, in many instances, more succinctly and profoundly than could be said again.

It is precisely this resolution to avoid replication that June cites as a reason for deciding not to write songs.

"The main reason is self criticism, an inability to come up with something that isn't derivative. I have ideas about what songs should be about, but I can't turn them into anything that I think is good enough. That's the problem when you've got people who are awfully good at writing songs around you, and you think, 'Well no, I'd rather sing something that is really well crafted rather than something that isn't very good but I'm going to sing it because I wrote it'. I have tried but they're no good. They never got as far as a tune, I don't think. But then I'll think, 'This really does deserve a song', so I'll ask somebody who's good to do it.

"A current example of that is Martin Simpson's fantastic song, 'Jackie And Murphy', about Jack Simpson and his donkey at

Gallipoli. I've been trying to make a song about that for years, but it just wouldn't come out right. And Martin has done a wonderful job on it. So I'll just provide the ideas and ask other people who are good songwriters to finish it off for me. Like the song 'Aqaba' (on the album of the same name), by Bill Caddick. I knew I wanted a song about Lawrence (of Arabia) and I knew some of the images that I wanted in it, but in a very marginal way. Bill turned it into an absolute masterpiece. Ken Hunt said to me, 'God help everybody else if you ever get round to writing songs!' But I never will, so they're safe – don't worry! I'm here to sing other people's songs."

Though singing other people's songs isn't always that straightforward. June has spoken about how, with some songwriters, the lyrics are so personal, it can be difficult for another singer to inhabit them. There has to be, she posited, "an element of detachment, I suppose, in the writing so that I can find a way to make the song my own".[81]

She elaborates: "A lot of modern songwriting is kind of stream of consciousness stuff, which works fine for the person who wrote it, but is, I would find, too diffuse and specific to that person. It really is a matter of saying, 'That's a good song when X sings it, but I don't think I could do anything with it'. I don't write songs, and I'm probably quite glad I don't in a way, but in another way I wish I did. So I'm acting as a kind of quality control agent for other people's work.

"A lot of the songs that I sang 30 or 40 years ago, I would probably only have understood later why I wanted to sing them, and quite a few of them I think, 'No, I don't know why I sang that'. A song is something that you're going to devote some energy to, and try to find a way to sing it, because quite a lot of songs I like I still don't know how to sing them, so I haven't tried them yet. It could take twenty years to work out the right way to do it. But the best ones, each time you sing that song, it's like it's the first time. And for the audience, however much they know it, it's like they're hearing it for the first time. And that is the greatness of a song and what I try and convey to listeners. There aren't that many of those, but they are there. It's just a matter of finding them, I suppose, or them finding me.

"You can only sing so many songs in your life and make them work. So I prefer to devote my energies into ones that I particularly like and think I can turn into mine, but it's totally subjective."

June has a reputation – and it's a reputation of which she's very aware – for being a singer of sad songs, as if this is a negative thing. But then society – or certainly western society – is largely intolerant of the minutiae of sadness, of the emotional forces that propel sadness, that conspire to contravene the omnipresent sense of optimism perpetrated and perpetuated by mass media. Yet the human condition is as predisposed to sadness as it is to the happiness or hopefulness we have been indoctrinated to believe is our default state. Into every life a little rain must fall. The trick is to let the rain soak you through rather than shelter from it.

The artistic gods of sadness – or, if you prefer, sorrow, misery, melancholy, gloominess, the blues – know this. They know that without suffering, there is no real joy. And those of us who gravitate to these gods know it too. Just as we know that sadness, experienced intimately – in the raw – begets perception. We don't listen to Frank Sinatra's *Only The Lonely* or Leonard Cohen, for example, because we want to be sad. We listen to them because we are sad and we want them to vivify our sadness. We want, in a sense, their empathy.

June Tabor has always understood the value – the potency – of sad songs, and she expounds: "When things aren't going right, that is when you need music in some form. Sometimes it can be just to reinforce your feeling you're not the only one to have made such a stupid mistake. That can make you feel better sometimes – 'I'm not the only one!'

"And when things are going right, you probably just want to get on with it. That's why I sing an awful lot of songs about love gone wrong. And if someone asks me, 'Don't you know any songs about love gone right?' I say, 'Of course I do, and here it is', as though there's only one. When things are going right, you might sing about it later.

"All these rules can be broken. There are always exceptions. But I think the disadvantages and mistakes and terrible parts of life often create the greatest and most moving pieces of art in whatever form you wish to see them, whether it's music or words or visual images. I do often get beaten with that stick, 'Oh, your songs are so dark', etc. etc., as though other art forms don't have that same bias. But they do. Name me a happy opera. It's there for a purpose, and usually it's because it's so strong."

It would be trite to imply that the sadness that has been a constant in June's music became more pronounced when she returned to recording with *Aqaba* in 1988, following the break-up of her marriage to David Taylor. But it's probably fair to say that she returned a different singer, changed by a very personal ordeal. She had turned her back on music and decamped to Penrith with Taylor.

"Why did I do it? The trouble was love. I fell in love with somebody in the hotel business who had always wanted their own restaurant,"[82] she told Peter Paphides of *The Guardian*.

Almost three decades later, her explanation for the sabbatical is considerably more prosaic. "There are only so many hours in a day, and when life turns into 24 hours a day running a restaurant, then something has to give. So at the time I had the restaurant I think I only did seven or eight gigs a year really and made one album. But when that ended... It was a bit like creating a dam, keeping all sorts of stuff back. And so when the dam got broken, goodness me, there was loads of energy and wanting to try all sorts of things. All those things that didn't get done during that time, suddenly demanded to be done. So, for the first time in my life, actually having a go at making music my full-time career. I'm still doing it, so I guess I got something right."

The return, June admits, "was daunting and difficult", but made easier by the fact that she surrounded herself with "good musicians" such as Martin Simpson, who had been with her from the beginning, and Huw Warren, who would replace Simpson as her principal accompanist.

"Again, because I hadn't made an album for several years, the songs were queuing up and saying, 'Come on, I want to be on it!' It was like doing the first album. There are so many things you want to put on it. And you have to leave things out. After that, it's not always so easy to find all the right songs. But that sort of gap, albeit in a haphazard way, they accumulated and were waiting to be sung."

§

June first met Simpson in 1977, a year after the release of his debut album, *Golden Vanity*, and shortly after her second album, *Ashes And Diamonds*.

"At that point she was still a professional librarian by trade, but she was being managed by a very nice chap called Paul Brown. He decided that he wanted to put her out on the road as a touring artist, despite the fact that it was few and far between because of her work. Nic Jones had played guitar on her records at that point, and he either wasn't available or didn't want to do the tour, so I got the call. I was delighted to do it, to put it mildly," says Simpson. "I'd bought all her records as they came out and I thought she was amazing. I thought she was an utterly, utterly wonderful singer, and had that ability to really make people cry, which I think is fantastic in a singer.

"I heard incredible quality, incredible emotional content. She lived in the songs. She inhabited the songs so well, and that emotional strength was just gigantic in her presentation. I loved it so much. And I also heard an incredible, in one sense, a huge discipline, a huge quality, and in another sense, a complete lack of discipline, a real wildness, which I knew was going to be fantastically stretching for me. And so it was.

"You listen to June sing and you realise that she's not really bound by strictures of time. So in a song she might sing one line in a regular fashion, but the next time around she might extend it considerably in order to make the words fit in properly. And as an accompanist you have got to be completely on top of that. So, basically, it really taught me so much about accompaniment. It was entirely about singing the song and making it work. She was at heart an unaccompanied singer. Those kinds of singers are able to be flexible, because there's nobody to accompany them. But then when you get to accompany that...! It's absolutely up to you to follow what the singer's doing. And that includes accompanying the lack of discipline, if you like."

An attentive, almost instinctive ear is required by the accompanist?

"You listen like fuck!" states Simpson with emphasis. "I didn't find it difficult, I actually loved it. It was one of the most educational and enjoyable parts of my entire career. We worked together basically for ten years from 1977 to 1987, when I left and went to the States. Since then, we've done bits and bobs. But that first four or five years was absolutely astonishing. Hugely important to me."

That period included *A Cut Above*, on which Simpson shares equal billing with June. The cover art features a photograph of the pair taken on a London bridge, the grubby River Thames below, the imposing Houses of Parliament beyond. What's most striking about the image though are June's thigh-length boots and the startling 1970s drag queen make-up, as she casually leans against the barrier and alongside a bearded Simpson (whose own fetching feminine boots elicit a slight elevation of the eyebrows), part-James Brolin, part-Peter Sutcliffe.

"We'd come up with all that material together, and almost all of the arrangements are essentially guitar-based, so it was just the right thing to do, to call it a June Tabor and Martin Simpson album," he explains.

A Cut Above would be the high water mark for Simpson in the context of his work with June. "That record was 'produced' by Paul Brown, he says. "The next two records, I suppose, were 'produced' by Andy Cronshaw, and I increasingly had less to do with the arrangements. And to be honest, it pissed me off. I didn't think it was a very wise way of operating in many ways. We're over it, you know, but at the time I was really pissed off. I was on my way to the States anyway. That was just something life presented me with, which was fantastic."

There were a couple of other albums – *Abyssinians* and *Aqaba* – before Simpson moved to Bloomington, Indiana, married

American singer Jessica Radcliffe (with whom he established the High Bohemia label) and finally settled in New York. His States odyssey lasted more than a decade, and included collaborations with Wu Man (*Music For The Motherless Child*) and Los Lobos' David Hidalgo (*Kambara Music In Native Tongues*). Back home in the UK since the 1990s, Simpson's solo career has burgeoned with albums such as *Prodigal Son, Purpose + Grace* and *Vagrant Stanzas*. But he remains a big fan of June's and hasn't ruled out the possibility of doing something together again in the future.

"When June and I stopped working together, basically she stopped working with guitarists at that point, and I always took that as being a massive compliment. We had a great relationship, and I brought material and ideas to her, and I was just there for her. Absolutely there for her.

"The mere sound of her voice is extraordinary. Since we started working together, her voice has dropped in pitch to an extraordinary degree. I think 'Strange Affair', the recorded version on *A Cut Above*, is probably in the key of C. Now she's doing it in G. That's a long drop.

"She has a sense of what she does now, which is more concrete than how she used to be. I think she's always had her voice. She's always been an extraordinary singer. She's worked with great, great jazz musicians, accompanying what she does, not always jazz accompaniment. I think she believes in herself. I think she believes in what she's doing and really sticks to her guns.

"There's nothing on the cards at the moment, but you just never know how things happen. I don't think it would be going back, I think it would be going forward. We're both arguably a lot more ourselves than we were then. I was 23, 24 when we first worked together. I basically rejected a rock'n'roll manager in order to accompany June Tabor. I was being managed by Tony Secunda, who was managing Steeleye Span and Motörhead and all kinds of stuff. Basically he was a twat, but he had vowed that he was going to make me a star. I went to him and said, 'I've got this opportunity to work with June Tabor'. And he said, 'Well, you fucking can't!' And I said,

'Excuse me?' He said, 'You're a fucking star – you don't play guitar for a chick'. My response was to go, 'Watch me'. That was the end of that. It was a great decision."

— Eleven —

The Voice Of Everywoman

¶

Four solo albums in almost three decades is a disproportionate and disappointing yield for Linda Thompson. An incurable throat condition has robbed her – and us – of a more prolific career since her split from Richard. Dysphonia is the medical term for an impairment in the ability to produce sounds using the vocal organs. The dysphonic voice – caused when an interruption in the vocal folds prevents them from vibrating normally during exhalation, resulting in muscle spasms – can be either hoarse, excessively breathy or harsh. Linda's condition began when she was pregnant with her first child, Muna.

"I would go to get a note out and there would be a delay, like a constriction. I put it down to pregnancy,"[83] she told the *Evening Standard* in 2003.

When Richard left her in 1982, she was "literally struck dumb. I had just had a third child, Kamila, a week earlier and I couldn't speak or even make a sound."[84]

She has tried speech therapy, psychotherapy and even Botox injections, none of which have worked long term. "I'm going to try Botox again. I haven't done it since it was in its infancy, and apparently it's more effective now. There is no cure though, as such," she tells me in an email. While I was writing this book, Linda's dysphonia was so bad, she could only correspond electronically.

That traumatic final US tour with Richard may have exacerbated the malady, although, according to the National Spasmodic Dysphonia Organisation in the United States, no scientific link has been established between stress and dysphonia. However, the Vanderbilt University Medical Centre, also in the States, claims "people will report that their symptoms worsen in the presence of stress, tension, emotional duress, fatigue or pressure".[85]

After the tour, Linda – who, by her own admission, was hooked "on anti-depressants and vodka" at the time – found herself nursed to relative health by Linda Ronstadt at the latter's home in Los Angeles. Then it was back home, back to the reality of single motherhood.

"I threw away the anti-depressants on the plane because I thought, 'I'm going back to the children now, I've had my lost weekend'. I cut down on the drinking. I didn't stop, I drank too much for a year after that."[86]

In London, it was John Tams whom Linda credited with essentially saving her life. He asked her to sing with Home Service – formed out of the ashes of The Albion Band – in a production of the medieval mystery plays. "Tams gave me a job at the National Theatre. Eight shows a week, two young kids and a newborn baby kept me busy, and got me through that time – as did my sainted mother,"[87] Linda recalled to Philip Ward.

The Mysteries ran for about a year, before Linda was courted by Mo Austin at Warner Brothers to do a solo album. *One Clear Moment* was produced by Hugh Murphy – the same Hugh Murphy who was Gerry Rafferty's producer, and who had worked on the initial aborted recording of what later became *Shoot Out The Lights*. Linda co-wrote most of the songs with Murphy's wife, Betsy Cook, a Kentucky native domiciled in the UK, whose previous sessions had included Rafferty, Squeeze and Frankie Goes To Hollywood.

"I had met Betsy years previously through Gerry Rafferty. We didn't click, then, years later, we did. I love her. She's a wonderful woman. It was really her to whom I gravitated, rather than the music. That came later."

One of the songs the pair wrote together was "Telling Me Lies", which would enhance Linda's songwriting reputation when Dolly Parton, Linda Ronstadt and Emmylou Harris featured it on their big selling *Trio* album in 1987. But not even that spur could deter Linda from describing *One Clear Moment* to Patrick Humphries as "eminently forgettable. What I should have done was get together a coterie of musicians that I was used to working with and done it that way."[88]

Simon Nicol, Linda's old Hokey Pokey sidekick, was "very taken with it. I love that record, to the point where I did a version of one of her songs on my first solo album ['Insult to Injury' on *Before Your Time...*]. That was really when the trouble started with her voice. She sang her way through that record, and after that, that's when the hysterical dysphonia really cut in. Had she not acquired that affliction, I'm certain that she would have been more motivated, more comfortable, in pursuing a career as a songwriter and she'd have been making more albums on the back of *One Clear Moment*, which would have had more continuity.

"It was a hobbling experience for her. But on the other hand, her life has become much larger than music. She's one of the most fulfilled people I know, and she's got that *savoir faire* really, rather than confidence. She has a brilliant mind and she finds good stimulation in everyday things. And she has excellent taste as well."

Linda lit out for Nashville to work on a follow-up to *One Clear Moment*, enlisting players like James Burton, Bruce Hornsby and Jennifer Warnes to play on it. But the dysphonia that had plagued her for more than a decade at that stage, brought the sessions to an end. She could hardly talk, let alone sing, and so decided to retreat from view. There wouldn't be another solo album until 2002, a gap of seventeen years, during which time Linda at least found domestic happiness with second husband Steve Kenis, an American businessman who moves in rarefied social milieu of Hollywood superstars such as Tom Cruise and Al Pacino.

There was the occasional project, among them an acting role in Pere Ubu frontman David Thomas' rogue opera, *Mirror Man*, commissioned by the South Bank in London and premiered at the Queen Elizabeth Hall in April 1998 as part of a the four-day festival, *David Thomas: Disastodrome! Mirror Man* pulled together lyrical and imagistic threads from Thomas' recordings and largely relied on improvisation and the personalities of the cast. Set in an abstract highway landscape among anonymous all-night coffee shops, bus stops, roadside detritus, apocryphal road signs, and flickering streetlights, Thomas described it as being "about places that don't exist and a collection of stories about the people who live there, abandoned by the future, forbidden access to the past, and set adrift in a mirage-like now."[89]

Richard and Linda Thompson albums were, Thomas says, "required listening in our circles in the early '70s, along with the Fairport Convention and *Henry The Human Fly* albums. In the Cleveland underground of the mid-'70s, bands in our circle performed Richard and Linda covers. I guess I first heard Linda on *Henry The Human Fly* before she was Linda Thompson.

"Her voice is gripping and immediate. I'm not a big fan of women's voices. In my grumpier moments I say women shouldn't be allowed to sing. And then I'd immediately say there are exceptions, prime among them Linda and Sandy Denny and Norma (Waterson) and Shirley and Dolly (Collins). From that list you can see how fond I am of English folk traditions. When I was young you listened to the Velvets, Stooges, MC5, Fairport, and Richard and Linda. Anyway, Linda's voice is always strong and assured and manly without those gross overtones some or many women apply to imitate male strength. Strength has always been encoded naturally in her voice, which is ironic considering how unsure she is about her singing ability!"

Thomas first met Linda in the early 1980s when he was asked by indie label Rough Trade to do a solo album. "Geoff Travis [Rough Trade founder] said to me, 'In your wildest dreams, if you could have any guitar player you wanted, who would it be?' Without hesitation I said, 'Richard Thompson'. He arranged for me to go to their house. I met her then."

Linda's version of how she came to be involved in *Mirror Man* – related to journalist Steve Lafreniere – had Thomas knocking on her front door and refusing to leave until she had agreed to perform the piece. "But I said I didn't think I could sing, and he said, 'Fine. Just speak the lyrics'."[90]

Thomas suggests this account is "a little overdrawn. I'm not the sort of person who will not leave until you say yes. I did say, 'If you can't sing, then just speak'. She was nervous about it. I assured her all she had to do was stand on stage and whatever she did would be good. Would be valuable and appropriate. I probably said something like, 'Don't think about it, just do it. Trust me.' I didn't know Linda all that well but I knew her voice. Her voice, as far as I am concerned, is the real Linda. Not the nerves, stage fright or uncertainty."

Thomas wanted Linda to play the part of a waitress in a diner because "she has the voice of everywoman. She has a universal quality that immediately supplies back story, without it having to be spelled out. She has depth. My admiration for her ability is hard to express."

The two haven't collaborated again since *Mirror Man*, though they did "some exploratory bits" for Thomas' improvisational group, David Thomas And Two Pale Boys.

"They were great. Despite her often stated feeling of inadequacy, she actually did very well just improvising. It would be a wonderful production. We work in opposite ways. She is very nervous about singing. I say, 'Just do it and don't think. Sing!' I care for her very much.

"There are two episodes I will take to my grave. One involves Linda. We were sitting at a piano at the South Bank during rehearsals for *Mirror Man*. She said to me, 'I wish I could sing like you'. I treasure that moment in the dark hours of the soul. I wish I could sing like her."

— Twelve —

Maddy The Motherfolker

♪

When Maddy Prior's son, Alex, was into rap music, he used to call her the motherfolker. In its profane variation, a term of endearment among rappers, Alex's witticism is more weighted with significance that perhaps even he intended – Maddy as the mother of English folk music, anyone? You could bulwark such a proposal with a solid argument based on her longevity alone, but the diversity of her oeuvre – always anchored in the traditional – is what really gives it ballast.

"Along with maybe June Tabor, Sandy Denny, Maddy is the first lady. No, The First Lady – of British folk music. Richard Thompson in a rather attractive frock," says Ian Anderson.

First there were the brace of albums with Tim Hart. Then came Steeleye Span – or rather, Steeleye Span came and went, and came again – and solo Maddy, which included a song with Dave Stewart and Annie Lennox (on *Going For Glory*'s "Deep In The Darkest Night"), and the conceptual *Arthur The King*. Add to that appearances on albums with Shirley Collins (*No Roses*), Ralph McTell (*Streets Of London*), Jethro Tull (*Too Old To Rock'n'Roll: Too Young To Die!*) and Mike Oldfield (*Incantations* and *Exposed*), and collaborations with Rev Hammer and The Levellers, and you catch my drift. Small wonder that, in 2001, she was awarded the MBE for services to folk music.

"It was really nice for my parents. And also, I think, it was a recognition of traditional music, finally. One or two people had got MBEs – Martin (Carthy) has got one. The Scots have got huge numbers of them. And it was like suddenly the English woke up to it. It's been interesting that over the last ten years there's been a rise in interest in traditional music in England. I don't think everybody is quite as sneery about Morris dancing as they were. It's gradually filtering through that this is what other countries spent quite a lot of money and time and energy on. Ireland has no problem with it. Scotland has no problem with it."

Maddy is right about the renaissance in traditional English music, which is probably at its most vibrant since the 1960s when she started out, with the likes of Eliza Carthy, Nancy Kerr, Bella Hardy and The Unthanks spearheading the new wave of women. Maddy herself has worked with some of the young ones, including Hannah James, singer, accordionist and clog dancer. James is one third of a trio alongside Maddy and Giles Lewin. They have already recorded an album, the well received *3 For Joy* (with plans for another), and done a couple of tours.

"My mum taught me to clog dance first, and then my dad used to run a folk festival in Derbyshire, so I've always been around it," says James of her immersion into traditional music. "I started to learn it a bit by default and then got more into it. When I was 11, I joined a young folk group in Stockport called The Fosbrooks (the Fosbrook Folk Education Trust). It's quite a unique thing really. It's run as a kind of club at school by a primary school teacher called Liza Austin Strange. They're all fantastic clog dancers and musicians."

As James began to engage more with "the rich history of recorded folk music", the names Steeleye Span and Maddy Prior would regularly appear on her radar.

"And actually, if you listen to the stuff that her and Tim Hart did – if you go to a folk club still, a lot of the songs that you hear being sung on floor spots, they're all songs and versions that they did back then. They really paved the way for a lot of the repertoire.

"I remember hearing her ornamentation, and the tenor and quality of her voice, and thinking that it was really sort of unique and it really lent itself to telling the stories of the songs. She was like no other singer I'd heard, really. Also, you can see how that has influenced a lot of other singers. She's been a massive influence on me, especially since we started performing together, because she's such an inspiring person. She never stops learning. She always wants to try new stuff out. She's very daring, actually – a good person to be around. She still sees herself as an artist who's learning and evolving all the time."

James jokes that Maddy is her "guru". They first met when James' ex-partner was working on John Spiers and Jon Boden's 10th anniversary album, *The Works*, in 2011. "Maddy was a guest on that album," James remembers. "Her and Rick (Kemp) came over one evening, and she recorded some vocals. Then we all went to the pub afterwards. It just so happened that there was a session going on in the local pub. They all know me quite well in there. Out came the bit of wood that they always get me to dance on, so I ended up doing some clog dancing. I didn't think anything else of it. She obviously clocked it. A few months later, she rang me out of the blue and asked me if I wanted to do a tour.

"I was pretty daunted. She did a trio project before with Benji Kirkpatrick and Giles Lewin, and I kind of thought I'd just be the replacement for Benji in that project and I'd probably have to learn a load of backing stuff for her songs, which is fine – I was really excited about that. Then I went to the first rehearsal and we all sat there, and Maddy said, 'Right then, what are we going to do?'! She really wanted to incorporate the stuff that me and Giles do as well, and make it into a trio, not just Maddy Prior with backing musicians. I think that's why the stuff on *3 For Joy* is so varied and a bit bonkers! Maddy knew I'd been to these ethno-music camps, where people from all over the world gather and teach each other music. I had a repertoire from those. And she'd done some Bulgarian singing with June (Tabor), and I'd learnt some Bulgarian songs, so we started there. She got excited about that, so we just delved into this mad repertoire I've got from all different places that I thought I'd never use in bands over here. The material was quite evenly spread among us.

"She's very humble. She's quite happy to give people the space to do their thing. A lot of people have said after the gigs that they were surprised how much limelight me and Giles get during the performance. They weren't expecting that – they were expecting Maddy to be at the forefront, whereas it's very even. If she appreciates what someone can do, she's quite happy to let them shine as part of a project. It's important to be able to take a back seat when you're collaborating. She's just so encouraging, no matter what you do or how way out it is. She's been pretty ground-breaking in her career. She's quite up for letting other people go for it and try new stuff."

The most valuable lesson James learned from time spent with Maddy both in the studio and on stage was "not to be shy of trying out new things. On the English folk scene you can get stuck in a rut of playing what you think audiences are going to go for, and not try to push the boundaries. On that tour I did a lot of things I thought people in this country wouldn't really appreciate listening to. And a lot of the time they're the things people respond best to. So I think you need to give audiences a bit of credit that they're going to listen and appreciate things that aren't maybe as conventional.

"One of the things I learned at these ethno-music camps was yodelling – I'm really into that vocal technique. Maddy really pushed me to do that in performance. It's not something people are used to hearing here, so I wasn't sure how they would respond to it, but actually I did it and it's probably the thing that people respond to most positively. It gets the most comments after the gigs. On the last tour we did a set of Austrian tunes with yodelling. She's been learning the technique as well, so we did a three-part yodelling harmony. She's always pushing me to do the next thing. There's a different style of yodelling that comes from Central Africa, a pygmy yodel. We were on stage at the last gig of the tour and someone shouted for more yodelling. So Maddy just made me do that, even though I'd never done it before! She's quite fearless as a performer, and she sticks to what she wants to do and hopes her audience will go with it."

Maddy has also been instrumental in stimulating James to pursue a singular path as a performer. She is one half of a duo with Bellowhead multi-instrumentalist Sam Sweeney, and is also a member of Lady Maisery, a vocal harmony trio with Hazel Askew and Rowan Rheingans, but now plans to augment both projects by doing her own thing.

"Maddy has been badgering me about doing some solo stuff. She thought the material I had could fill a solo gig. In the end she gave me a push and asked me to do a support for Steeleye Span, so I did my first ever solo gigs supporting them."

Maddy downplays her mentoring role in James' development. It's not such a big deal – more a case of, why wouldn't she do it? "It's such a nice thing to do. Hannah's just brilliant," enthuses Maddy. "She's incredibly skilled. I'm very impressed by skill, because it's not what I've got. Now that I'm getting into the teaching thing, I'm getting more into this idea of passing things on. I think you do when you get to a certain point.

"I never make decisions – they're sort of made for me. I always assume things are going to work. If I think of an idea, I want it to work, and I want it to work in a way that I think it will. That's what drives me more than anything – whatever I do, I want it to be good. I want it to be a good body of work. But then I don't get over precious about it. If it's not as good as I'd like it to be, that doesn't stop me. It can stop people because they get too particular about it, wanting it to be accurate and precise, brilliant and perfect. I don't get that. It's like vulnerability, for instance – like being terrified on stage. Most people desperately don't want that to be seen. And I've spent my whole career worrying about that. But actually, having seen Annie Briggs, who was one of the most terrified performers I've ever seen, it was incredibly engaging. You didn't necessarily think she was terrified, but she was vulnerable. And that vulnerability was evident, whether you thought of it as nervousness. Perfection is not my thing. I want it to be good and I want it to be robust. I've come to the conclusion that's probably a good word for me – robust. I like to try and be honest as well, but it doesn't always work.

"The skill that some of these youngsters have got now is incredible. I have these ideas but it's a bit prog rock, probably. Steeleye are playing a big prog rock festival next year. In a way that's what we've always probably been, so it's kind of interesting to have found what we maybe are. The thing about prog rock is the ideas are strong in it. Songs, I want them to say a bit more than perhaps they're set up to do. Bellowhead are good at picking songs that mean something, that have some content and guts. A lot of the youngsters now, when they started out, were all singing the Victorian ballads, which our lot didn't really do that much of – we thought they were a bit naff. But now I think they're changing. It was all very left wing when we were coming up. They're not particularly political now, but they're more socially aware. It goes in slightly different ways. Art is trying to do something with limits, but pushing those limits as far as you can. You have to have some kind of discipline, because it doesn't work if you don't."

Another of the younger ones is Maddy's own daughter, Rose Kemp, who performed with Steeleye Span while still a teenager, and has fused her folk lineage with other genres on the albums, *A Hand Full Of Hurricanes*, *Unholy Majesty* and *Golden Shroud*. She released her debut album at the age of 18, much to her proud mum's delight, who says: "She should have had an album out when she was 15 because she could do it then, but actually she's come on a storm since. She's gained so much confidence. Rick (Kemp) has been a great mentor for her. They've got a similar musicality. They're absolutely certain about where the beat is, and that sort of thing. There's a surety about their musicality that I don't have. It's a different sort of confidence with the music. What I do is much more intuitive and vague. They're much more specific and they know what they're doing more than I do."[91]

Rose has recently taught extreme singing "for vocalists who want to explore or improve the heavy side!"[92]

Maddy too is a teacher, at the Stones Barn centre of creative expression and excellence in Cumbria (which she established in 2003, and where she is helped out by Rose), running courses on singing, meditation, performance and, ahem, cookery.

"I live remote, in English terms. I'm ten miles from the nearest shop. My mother came to live with me. She'd been in towns all her life. I thought I'd have to do something to make it not quite so remote for her. And so I decided to do some courses. I didn't know if it would work or not. It kept me home a bit, which was the other thing, so I was around the mother. That was good for three or four years, and then she passed on. The courses continued and have established themselves in my life for the last ten or eleven years. One of the things we've realised is that huge numbers of people want to sing, and that is evident by the massive rise in choirs, television programmes about singing – it's all going mad everywhere. There are people who say, 'You wouldn't want to hear me sing', 'I'm tone deaf', all these things. And I say, 'Somebody told you probably when you were about 9 or 10 that you couldn't sing. And you'll know who it was'. And they do. That's usually the reason they don't sing. It's tragic really that it takes very little to stop people singing.

"I do a course called 'Singing for the Uncertain'. People come to those classes and then they go away and join choirs. It's been incredibly delightful to run these courses. I'm not a born teacher. Strangely enough, I'm now doing a course in Denmark to learn to sing and to learn how to teach it. I'm learning the mechanics of singing. And also, to get that back again, because you lose it if you don't use it. There's a system called CVT in Denmark – Complete Vocal Technique – that goes right across all genres. It has been an incredible shock to the system, because I've had to try to learn other ways of singing, which is really weird. I go over there six times a year for three years."

§

Maddy has never stopped developing her voice, mining it to discover untapped resources, new ways of expressing the language of heart and mind. The unfamiliar doesn't faze her but presents itself as an opportunity – a challenge to be embraced. After all, what could be more challenging than for an untrained singer to join her voice with the schooled voices of The Carnival Band, an early music group whose repertoire focuses on popular music from the 16th and 17th centuries? Formed by Andy Watts, principal bassoon in the Orchestra Of The Age Of Enlightenment, and Giles Lewin when both were members of The Medieval Players touring theatre company in the 1980s, they define themselves as "five musical explorers, five voices, 25 instruments, five dozen styles of music and 500 fresh ideas for music making, combining music from across the centuries with sounds from around the world in an irreverently joyous mix".[93]

The Carnival Band's roots can be traced to the pre-Lenten street festivals of Medieval Europe, "which gave communities licence to 'turn the world upside down'. We do just that with our music. We've invented Macedonian reggae, turned a renaissance chanson into a Piaf-inspired drag act, paired Noel Coward with James Brown, flavoured a traditional English carol with Cajun spice..."[94]

The Carnival Band's relationship with Maddy goes back to 1984. "A [BBC] Radio 2 producer called John Forrest takes the credit for teaming us up," says Watts. "He had the idea of recording five carols to be broadcast one each day in a week in December. We recorded the tracks in a village hall near Carlisle with a BBC mobile unit. A few years later, I asked Maddy if she'd like to do an album of similar material, and that was *A Tapestry Of Carols*."

According to Maddy, The Carnival Band promised the carols would be "all the normal ones, so I thought, 'OK', came to look at the material and knew about four. It was their idea of ordinary, and a medieval player's idea of ordinary isn't mine. But I learned some wonderful songs."[95]

"Angels In The Realms Of Glory" is one of the carols Maddy particularly remembers. "It was done in a Cajun style, very fast, very high. And I thought, 'This is different!' We did it the next year. And I said, 'We could do an album, couldn't we?' Nobody was doing Christmas albums of traditional carols. So we said we'd do carols that everybody knows, and they proceeded to send me a tape with songs I'd never heard in my life! But they were beautiful."

Maddy's lack of training has never been a problem for her as part of The Carnival Band, as Watts explains: "We play a lot by ear, we improvise, so reading conventional notation is only part of what we do. It's not a problem. Notation, guitar tabs, mp3 files, smartphone recordings – they are just tools to help us work quicker and remember stuff. We enjoy working in different musical worlds. Giles Lewin, our fiddle player, was a member of Bellowhead for a while, Steve Banks and Steno Vitale are in the folk rock band, Chanter, and Jub, our bass player, does a lot of contemporary music."

Maddy, though, does admit she was daunted by The Carnival Band at first: "That's a whole different world. They're all readers and they're all classically trained. It was kind of scary, really. They kind of go through something twice and they've got it, whereas I'd be in a situation where we'd rehearse for days, going over and over songs, so they'd go in almost by osmosis. I didn't have to sit and learn the songs. By the time they'd arranged the songs, because we were making it up as we went along, I'd know the song by the end of that time, because it would go in by repetition. We'd keep going over the song until we got it right. Whereas they would write it and once they'd got the arrangement, that was it. I was going, 'No, no – I haven't got this yet!'

"They are brilliant. And they're great lads. All that learning sits very lightly on them. Andy, who's the MD if you like, he does Glyndebourne and he's a tutor at the Royal College – quality stuff. I've worked a lot with Giles, who's a fantastic musician. I always think of Giles as being slightly understated. He's not a flashy player but he really knows his stuff. We used to do pantomimes and all kind of nonsense with them as well. I've never been limited by taste!"

For Watts, Maddy perfectly complements the range of The Carnival Band's instruments – as well as the conventional, their sonic cornucopia features the historical, such as shawm and Flemish bagpipes, and the exotic in the djembe – along with their sense of minimalism. "As a singer, she has a wonderful unique sound and an ability to communicate a song with clarity and conviction. She is up there with the greats. As a collaborator, she is hard working, generous, enthusiastic, ready to learn, eager to try new musical experiences. On tour she is one of the band and we feel we're working with her, not just backing her. It's a very happy partnership.

"Maddy has encouraged and helped us artistically in many ways, but I'd single out our singing and songwriting. We are primarily instrumentalists, but she has always been enthusiastic about our harmony singing and even our solo singing. We are much better vocalists thanks to her. In the early days we never wrote our own material, but Maddy gave us the encouraging push we needed to write. As well as that she has taught us a huge amount of stagecraft and recording know-how, just by working together."

Maddy and The Carnival Band have recorded nine albums together, the last of which was 2007's *Ringing The Changes*.

"We are still touring the *Carols And Capers* show every other year, and we change it every time to keep it fresh," says Watts. "Maddy has invited several of us to lead workshops on her Stones Barn courses. We're all busy on different projects so we can't get together very often, but we're still finding fresh material and coming up with new ideas. On our last tour we set up carnival community choirs in three of the venues, which gave the gigs a whole new dimension.

"The Carnival Band is about to embark on a three-year project to record the 100 top hits of the 17th century as part of a research programme based at Queen's University Belfast. They are broadside ballads, a cross between a tabloid newspaper and a hit song. Maddy has agreed to record some of the ballads with us. Maybe an album will emerge but initially the recordings will be held on a public access website so anyone can hear them for free."

❡

And so Maddy's metamorphosis continues, unimpeded by her advance into her late sixties, a period when many would elect to indulge themselves in past accomplishments. But whatever the nature of the next thing, where it takes her, she stays faithful to the tradition that was her first love as a young girl, when friends "thought I was bonkers doing this English stuff". If she was ever bonkers, it was always in a good way – and always in thrall to the music.

Maddy The Motherfolker

"Everybody will have all kinds of ideas about who I am and what I do, depending on what they've seen or what they've read. That's what live gigs are all about, seeing who the person is. But I think if the material's not good enough, it doesn't matter how good you are. Then it just becomes about how skilled you are. There are some incredibly skilled players, but if the material doesn't capture you... Someone like Phil Cunningham [Scottish folk musician and composer] writes brilliant tunes and they've got something in them, some content, that makes you just want to sit and listen. But if he was just playing other material, it wouldn't interest me. So being a great player isn't what it's about for me. But then for some people it is. That's the great thing about music – you can find something in it for everyone.

"I wanted to do good work. I wanted for the work to be appreciated. There was never a big umbrella principle. I used to love doing interviews with Bob [Johnson] and Tim [Hart], because they had this great idea about what we were doing, and I just always thought we staggered from song to song! And as they fell together that was what made it what it was, a kind of a cumulative bunch of minutiae rather than an overall scheme.

"Traditional music incorporates everything. All life is in the songs – the social and the political. It works in my life, and I find it incredibly interesting to do."

Thirteen

God Broke The Mould

♪

While it wasn't exactly a comeback, the release of *Aqaba* in 1988 did represent a coming back of sorts for June Tabor after a five-year recording hiatus. It also represented a changing of the guard in terms of accompanists. Martin Simpson, her sideman on *A Cut Above* and *Abyssinians*, had moved to America. He did appear on *Aqaba* – playing guitar and baritone guitar on "Where Are You Tonight, I Wonder", and mandola on the title track – but this would be his final collaboration with June until 2003's *An Echo Of Hooves*. Huw Warren, who contributed piano to "The Old Man's Song (Don Quixote)", was soon to become a regular fixture on her albums and in live performance.

Swansea-born Warren began as a cellist in the West Glamorgan Youth Orchestra and an organist in the working men's clubs of South Wales, before going on to study piano at the University of London under the innovative John Tilbury, and later at the Guildhall School of Music and Drama. He was co-founder (with Mark Lockheart, Dudley Phillips and Martin France) of jazz quartet Perfect Houseplants, and produced joint projects with early music practitioners Andrew Manze, Pamela Thorby and The Orlando Consort, as well as releasing five albums of his own material on jazz imprint Babel.

"*Aqaba* is the transition between working with Martin and working with Huw," says June. "I had actually started working with Huw as part of the second Silly Sisters band. Martin was almost signing off, and off to America, and Huw was just beginning to work with me. So it's an extremely significant album in terms of the accompanists, without whom I would not be.

"The art of accompaniment is a very, very difficult and specialised thing, particularly when you're not accompanying yourself. You know when you're going to breathe and pause, and that sort of thing, but to accompany someone else and get it right, is an exceptionally underrated ability. And certainly during the time I was working with Martin, he had it. And now Huw has it, quite extraordinarily.

"And it's so important, it really is. The only way A can accompany B with no previous experience, is if everything happens exactly the same and in time, and frequently – it can happen, and it's happened to me – the accompanist will tell the singer what to do, and I don't like that. It doesn't work. It can work for other people, it doesn't work for me. I have to be the one who is leading and phrasing and all that, and the accompanist has to be an absolute fraction of a second behind me – not so as you'd notice. So if I make a mistake, they understand that and they don't go straight on!"

June believes that as an accompanist – her accompanist – Warren has no equal. "He has incredible sympathy, empathy, anticipation, understanding of the way I think and what I want to achieve, plus the fact that his instrument is an orchestra in itself. Just having seen the way that Huw has changed and developed and expanded as a pianist in the 26, 27 years we've been working together, is also extraordinary. He is unique. God broke the mould when he made Huw. He is amazing and there is nobody quite like him."

❡

Before linking up with June, Warren's only previous venture into folk music was as a member of Pyewackett, "whom I toured with for the British Council when Bill Martin (their keyboardist) didn't want to work abroad. When June and Maddy Prior decided to revisit their Silly Sisters collaboration in '87 they both were keen on working with musicians who had no previous connection, and I think it was Pyewackett's Ian Blake who put my name forward to June and Maddy. We ended up rehearsing at Maddy's house in

Cumbria for a week with Breton guitarist Dan Ar Braz, and I think after the very first day of rehearsing, June mentioned to me that her long time accompanist, Martin Simpson, was moving to the States and did I fancy doing some gigs as a duo?!

"I still remember the first Silly Sisters gig at the Purcell Room (on London's Southbank) in the autumn of 1987, and then subsequently our first duo gig at Northwich – the local folk club, I think – sometime in 1988. We'd worked on so many songs, and never timed anything, so we just played the lot – it was quite a long gig!"

Warren had seen June perform just the once, a brief set many years previously with Andrew Cronshaw. So what was it about her that convinced him they could form a successful creative relationship?

"That most incredible commitment to the lyric, to the storytelling and the inexplicable dramatic power that this unleashes," says Warren. "I've always played a wide variety of music, and in 1988 was already making many collaborations in the jazz, experimental and World music scenes, so collaborating with June seemed also like an amazing way of learning about traditional repertoire as well as the contemporary song material that she introduced me to."

After Simpson, Warren believes he brought a "breadth of style and concept of the role of the accompaniment", yet he also admits to having taken "several things from Martin. I saw their final gig at the Half Moon, Putney, and it really was an object lesson in accompaniment. For instance, a really simple example was the treatment of very simple diatonic harmony – harmony fundamentally based in one key – without it ever sounding simple! I think I managed to absorb a little of this and add my own wider approach, including the orchestral possibilities of the piano. Repertoire-wise, I think it was also the first time that June had worked with someone who knew some of the songs from the jazz world – especially Sinatra – which she had learned by (her description) osmosis."

June's lack of musical training has never posed a problem for Warren, just as it hadn't with Simpson. "The definition of a 'musician' is often just in the descriptive language," says Warren. "So while talking about musical definitions was not always possible, there was generally not a lot of this kind of conversation. It either worked or it didn't, and if it didn't we would just move on, or revisit later. The fact that we have always learned new material by June singing it to me unaccompanied, has led to a very strong way of working. I have said many times in interviews that by the time I get to hear a song, it already sounds amazing. My job is often not to make it sound better, but just to stay out of the way, in a way that will eventually give even more dramatic and emotional impact to the performance. It's definitely understated, both in emotional terms and also technically in musical terms – for example, allowing the voice to dictate the rhythm and finding certain chords where the voice hits the crucial note and the piano avoids.

"I think it's a combination of really understanding the emotional basis of the songs. We spend time discussing the lyric – and often this is a multi-layered interpretation, much like a great short story – and everything else then is developed from this. There's no point in using clever or complex musical statements if they don't support the fundamental emotional approach of the arrangement. This having been said, I really feel that the arrangement should have a life and story of its own, in the same way that a simplistic film score merely mirrors the emotions of the picture, whereas a more interesting score can also hint at a story of its own, or maybe another way of looking at the same story."

When two artists have enjoyed such an enduring association, inevitably over time they develop a finely-honed sense of intuition. So finely-honed, in fact, that each can almost project themselves into the other's mindset – each knows what the other will bring to the song and each knows what the other wants.

"But I think that all my musical relationships – with Maria Pia de Vito, Iain Ballamy, Mark Lockheart and Peter Herbert – are also like that!" says Warren. "With June we both have the understanding and trust to know that the barest and most minimal arrangements can make the most devastating emotional impact, and I have the freedom to comment on the lyric in my intros, links or outros. I think we share that desire to serve the song. That's why she only picks great songs!"

When June is the singer serving the song, the song becomes a layered entity because of what she brings – what Warren identifies as "intensity, commitment to the lyric, passion, humour, knowing exactly what she wants from her voice and an intuitive and indescribable authoritative quality that enables her to have such a transformative effect on the audience. I think it is fundamentally about sharing the things that she feels strongly about via the medium of songs. Sometimes we've played an intense set, and it feels like the rest of the world has stood still whilst we live entirely in the worlds of songs."

❡

Melodeon player Andy Cutting is in demand not just among his traditional music peers – having worked with Chris Wood, Martin Simpson and Kris Drever – but also in the rock and pop medium. He has recorded with Sting and former Dire Straits bassist John Illsley, and sat in with The Who at an acoustic concert in aid of the Teenage Cancer Trust. John McCusker, himself no mean musician, reckons he has "learned loads just by listening to Andy play", [96]while to Martin Simpson he is "the consummate accompanist, harmonically, rhythmically and melodically, and an exquisite soloist".[97] June goes even further, equating the magic that Cutting wrings from his instrument to "going through the wardrobe and finding Narnia. His music is glorious, joyful, moving, subtle, emotionally charged, a totally spellbinding experience that is never long enough."[98]

He made his recording debut with June on her 1994 album, *Against The Streams*, and has since graced *Aleyn*, *At The Wood's Heart*, Apples and *Ashore*.

"June had seen me play in a duo with Chris Wood," Cutting says. "When she was putting the songs together for *Against The Streams*, there was a song written by Les Barker ('The Turn Of The Road') that she thought would really suit me, so she came to a concert I was playing and at the end came and asked me if I would play on the record. I was deeply flattered that she'd asked me, so I trusted that she heard in my music something that would work well with her singing." And Cutting was very familiar with June's singing, having seen her many times when, as a young boy, his parents, fervent folkies, took him to several festivals.

In his role as accompanist, he listens intently and endeavours to grasp "the mood and spirit of the songs. The more we have done over the years, the better we seem to get at it. June's a great musician. You don't have to play an instrument to be a musician. June generally doesn't say much as far as what she wants on a song, unless it's not working. Sometimes we'll try variations on the instrumentation. I think she trusts us all to adapt and respond accordingly."

Cutting identifies June's instinctive capacity "to get inside the song and convey the story to the listener" as being the overriding factor that makes her such a compelling singer. There are, he suggests, "few singers who can do that so brilliantly. June is unique and pretty much without equal in terms as a singer of folk music."

¶

Les Barker originally hails from Manchester but is now Welsh. He once held down a sensible job as an accountant before, as he tells it, becoming a professional idiot as assistant to Mrs Ackroyd, "a small hairy mongrel who lay around in folk clubs, bit people and became famous". A poet and parodist, Barker has written a staggering 77 books – spawning several folk heroes, including Jason and the Arguments, Cosmo The Fairly Accurate Knife Thrower and Spot of the Antarctic – and, as leader of The Mrs Ackroyd Band (formed after the demise of the aforementioned mutt, Mrs Ackroyd), produced a spate of albums, on one of which, 1989's folk opera, *The Stones Of Callanish*, a certain June Tabor makes her debut as a member of the ever-evolving ensemble.

Barker recounts how The Mrs Ackroyd Band came into being: "Back in 1987, I was making a live album at Bromyard Festival, and wanted to include a few parodies I'd written. I'd just made an album with Steve and Lesley Davies, so I recruited them and we added a few extra members on site. Everybody enjoyed the experience, so we decided to carry on.

"The important thing for me was the quality of the music. I take as much care writing comedy as I do with a serious song, and the same applies to the performance. When Chris Harvey joined the band, he would build up orchestral arrangements instrument by instrument. The people who've performed with the band have all been exceptional musicians apart from me."

June got involved with Mrs Ackroyd, says Barker, "the same way that other people have. All the musical albums I've made have included friends from the folk scene. And in the early days we'd recruit other musicians when we appeared at festivals. June doesn't do a lot of festivals, but when she did, she was happy to be part of it. She's been including one or two of my comedy songs in her own performances for years – performed the way they should be performed, properly – so it was only natural she should be there. She must feel that it adds to the balance of the evening. A performance should include light and dark, and she understands that."

Such understanding is required by June's audience. However, there are those among the broader folk audience who, blinded by a misguided preconception of her as some sort of purveyor of the portentous, channelling tormented narratives, are confounded by June the jester. She relates an especially amusing anecdote about singing with The Mrs Ackroyd Band at the Sidmouth Folk Festival.

"I was singing 'The Trains Of Waterloo' with Lesley Davis – a parody of the 'The Plains Of Waterloo' about a commuter. It's a typical Les song – when it starts off, you think it's the original and then it turns into something else completely. My friend, Joan, was in the audience and she's standing next to a couple. The bloke says to the girl, 'Who's that on stage next to Lesley Davis?' And his girlfriend says, 'It's June Tabor'. And he said, 'It can't be – I've seen her before and she's really miserable!' Joan was stuffing her handkerchief into her mouth to stop laughing!"

June is a big fan of Barker's parodies. She wishes more people could hear them. "They can be overlooked. A lot of what Les used to write could never be recorded. Many of his songs that we do in our live set are parodies of standards. You can't record those without getting the weight of Warner Bros or whoever coming down on you like a ton of bricks. They don't approve of that kind of thing. Something like 'Send In The Cones', Les' parody of 'Send In The Clowns'... (at this juncture, June proceeds to sing it for me, word and note perfect). The only ones that can be recorded are when they're set to traditional tunes. Some of his stuff about Bush and global warming, oh, magnificent!"

Barker seldom writes with singers in mind, though "The January June" (composed to the melody of "January Man" and featured on The Mrs Ackroyd Band's *Gnus And Roses*) was an exception.

"One or two songs have come out of suggestions from June or Mark [Emerson, June's partner in life and art and another regular accompanist]", says Barker.

"Generally I write because I want to say something, or because there's a tune I want to do something with. Sometimes I can hear a specific singer's voice as I'm writing, but that's just part of the writing process. Once I've finished a song, it's there for the rest of the world to do with as they wish. At some point, I learn that June's singing it, and at some later point, I learn she's recorded it, and it's always a nice surprise."

Barker suffered a heart attack in 2008, after which he quit the band, given that it was "the most complicated thing I did. Chris Harvey, Alison Younger and Hilary Spencer have carried on The Mrs Ackroyd Band as a trio, and it works very well. Over the last few years I've been learning Welsh, and I now have a Welsh band. I'm not in that either! It's a very satisfactory arrangement. I've no idea what's coming next, but something will."

¶

If The Mrs Ackroyd Band revealed June's inner clown, 1990's *Freedom And Rain* with Oyster Band, gave vent to her inner punk. The Oyster Ceilidh Band were formed around 1976, the "Oyster" bit derived from their early association with Whitstable, the Kent town renowned for the quality of its oysters. They morphed into Oyster Band at the outset of the 1980s, self-releasing a series of albums on their Pukka Music label, including *English Rock'n'Roll: The Early*

Years 1800-1850, *Lie Back And Think Of England* and *Liberty Hall*. *Freedom And Rain* was actually their last album as Oyster Band before the subtle name change to Oysterband.

"Our paths had crossed a few times, meeting at festivals and things, so they knew who I was and I knew who they were," says June of what, on the surface, seemed like an unlikely alliance, but what was, on record and in performance, anything but. "We got talking in the Dove at Sidmouth, a pub where all the musicians used to go because there was no music in there, so you could actually get to sit down and talk and you could hear yourself! They said, 'We want to do something different. It would be great if we could find' – because it was when 10,000 Maniacs were quite big – 'somebody like Natalie Merchant and just float the voice over what we do, someone who'll throw themselves about on stage a bit'. I said, 'Well, I could maybe do the voice, but I'm not sure about throwing myself about on stage!'

"This was around the time when the restaurant finished and I was trying to decide what to do with my life. All these musical ideas were flooding in, and this was one of them. So we went away and thought about it for quite a long time, and thought about possible songs that might work. Then we got back in touch and decided to get together and try it without committing ourselves too much, or without telling anybody what we were going to do, or what we might want to do. We worked on a few songs and it did seem as though it had something going for it. And it all developed from that. Only then did they work hard on the songs and eventually make the album and then do a tour. We went to America and had all sorts of adventures."

Oyster Band knew June's reputation before getting to know June. They may have appeared on the same festival bill a few times, "but we wouldn't claim to have known her any better than to smile and say hello to", says the band's fiddle player, Ian Telfer. "I guess socially we met in the summer of '89 at Sidmouth Festival. I think we were introduced by Ian Anderson, editor of *fRoots* magazine. I have a vague memory of saying, 'Oh, introduce us to June'.

"She was a very glamorous figure then, and we were delighted to find out that she was very approachable. We sat down and we got stuck into the drink. Our singer, John, likes to say, 'We woke up in the morning and found that we'd made an album!' "It was almost as quick as that that we decided to do one. June has the image of doing fairly severe and heavily acoustic stuff. But actually, she's quite open to all kinds of other things if the material is right or the people are right. And a couple of drinks later we were busy plotting and planning. And in the late autumn of that year she came down and visited a house where I was living at the time, and she brought about half the material for an album, and we suggested the other half, and I personally wrote another song at the last minute just to make the numbers up. And we recorded in the spring of 1990."

It was the attraction of opposites.

"At that time Oysterband was a good deal punkier than it subsequently became," explains Telfer. "We were very fond of making a noise and had lots of energy. She had this very cool delivery and, of course, a ravishingly beautiful voice. We thought that somehow there's got to be something piquant that we can make out of these two things, and she thought so to.

"We worked at a studio in Southall. We worked in the studio by day, and by night lots of Indian musicians came in and did their thing. Each morning we would come in and find the ashtrays overflowing, the waste paper bin full of empty half bottles of whiskey and stuff like that. And we thought, 'Ah, not so different!' We went for the option of a cheap-ish studio for the longest time.

"We didn't start with a huge number of more songs than went on the album. In a way the choice of songs is all terribly obvious, in as much as we were covering Richard Thompson, covering Shane MacGowan, covering Billy Bragg. These were the name songwriters in that kind of world at that time. What I've discovered from that subsequently is that it's quite alarming what June will sing if the wind's blowing in the right direction. She sang, I believe, in a rock covers band when she was at school, and anything that comes from Grace Slick, that epoch, she'll happily pick up a microphone and have a go at."

Before Oysterband, June had never fronted a proper band. By the time she had reunited with the Oysters – as June affectionately refers to them – in 2011 for *Ragged Kingdom*, everyone concerned had, says Telfer, "all learnt an immense amount about how to do these things. It was so much easier – and it was so much easier on stage as well. In 1990, we learned the hard way how to do soundchecks with June. This time round, we were totally on top of that."

June and the Oysters did tour in support of *Freedom And Rain*, but Oysterband were so busy with other projects that any notion of an immediate follow-up "kind of slid away in the distance", as Telfer tells it. "We had a very young record company, Cooking Vinyl. They were very lucky – the first album they put out was Michelle Shocked's *Texas Campfire Tapes*, so unlike any record company starting out, they instantly had a bit of money in their pocket. And Oysterband's first album, first non-self-made album, was the second one. So we had the benefit that they were making rapid connections with record companies and agencies all over the world. Our work schedule at that time was clinically insane – it was like Bournemouth on Wednesday, Belfast on Friday and Seattle on Monday, and it went on like that for months.

"It's not like we had careers in all that many countries, but Cooking Vinyl had links to companies in other countries who were keen to make it possible for us to visit. The June thing, it kind of just slid away, we were so stupidly busy. We went running around in circles for four or five years. When we first went to the States with June in '91, there was a big head of steam of expectation of American folkies, who really wanted to see this novel proposition, June with an electric band. It got a very interested response. After that, she went several more times. But then, as happened for Oysterband separately, it kind of tailed off. By the time we got to the West Coast, we played McCabe's in Los Angeles, a very small but high status venue – it's a very good place to play if you're coming in for the first time. We had Jackson Browne and Leonard Nimoy and all sorts of people in the audience, along with all the folkies from LA and San Francisco. It was never so easy again!"

The reunion on an eclectic collection of traditional and contemporary covers from "Bonny Bunch Of Roses" to Joy Division's "Love Will Tear Us Apart", came about at the urging of others.

"We stayed friends, and still are good friends, and occasionally I'd do one or two things with them," says June. "Then, twenty years after the first album, we did a session – a folk benefit at the Roundhouse – and it seemed so good playing together, and one or two people said, 'You really ought to do another album together'. So we decided to have a think about the sort of material we might want on it, because it's only going to be as good as the material. We know we can play together but it's got to be the right songs. And again, it was this process of everybody contributing ideas. This was going to be a good thing to do twenty years on. We were all older and wiser and smarter, just doing things in a slightly different way. And it worked really, really well."

The Roundhouse date was a benefit for *fRoots* magazine, whose editor Ian Anderson put the bill together. Telfer remembers, "He said, 'Right, I get to pick what happens, because it's my party. Would you do two or three songs?' We did. And, as June said, it was terrific. We thought, 'Actually, these are good songs'. In the intervening years we'd maybe played four or five times together at intervals, so we didn't have to blow as much rust off the material as you might expect. And some of the things that we really enjoyed were easy to remember anyway."

When Oysterband told their agent of their intention to do another album with June after 21 years, the agent's waggish reply, according to Telfer, was, "Oh, are we doing any material from this millennium?!' I said, 'Nope!' Whereas before we attempted very contemporary covers, this time around only P.J. Harvey made the cut ('That Was My Veil'). June could fully understand P.J. Harvey's angle on stuff. But some of the other stuff we suggested, that we thought would do perfectly for June, she didn't care to do. There were two winnowing processes that went into the material for both of those albums."

The winnowing process for *Ragged Kingdom* was often painstaking. Not everyone was in concert when it came to song selection.

"We'd had a slow turnover of personnel in the intervening time, and not everybody that was now playing with Oysterband had actually fully understood what June did or where she came from," says Telfer. "So we had a lot of failed suggestions for material. At one point I had 36 songs written on a piece of paper, and playfully asked Topic Records if they'd like a triple album. I got a dusty answer! We got it whittled down to a dozen and went to Rockfield near Monmouth and it didn't take long.

"John (Jones, Oysterband singer) had had that ornamental list of something we could one day do with June if there was ever a call for it. He sort of thinks occasionally about duets and female singers and so forth. One of them was 'Love Will Tear Us Apart'. There is a real song in there. It's an intensely romantic song. June took to it immediately. We realised when we slowed it down, she really got her teeth into it. It's not a duet in the original version. I thought we had done something quite original with it. And the words really stand up to greater exposure to being drawn out a little. When I Googled it at the time, there were 88 cover versions, most of which are crap. But I really feel we did one of two or three best cover versions."

June acknowledges that the *Ragged Kingdom* sessions were, at times, chaotic. But great beauty, as exemplified in this instance, often emerges from chaos.

"When we were doing the album, of course everyone's got their own ideas about what should and shouldn't be," says June. "Al Scott, who played on the album and produced it, he said, 'Are you finding this difficult?' I said, 'Yeah, well when we do an album – me and Huw, Mark and Andy – we know what we're doing before we start, and I have the final say!'" Relinquishing her veto though didn't mar her enjoyment of the project.

"It's a different performance. And in some ways it isn't. Certainly the gigs we did this last time with *Ragged Kingdom*, there was a bit more of me in it than the last album, but then I probably didn't know who 'me' was when we did *Freedom And Rain*. We sat one night at Ian's house and put *Freedom And Rain* on the stereo. We stopped eating and said, 'Bloody hell, wasn't it fast?!' But it's a classic album. You can tell on *Ragged Kingdom* it's the same people and the same band, but there's that twenty year gap and that development that's occurred in the way that the music is presented."

The folk world fully embraced *Ragged Kingdom*. Robin Denselow's review in *The Guardian* applauded its energy "along with the desire to startle and experiment... a new maturity and emotional depth, and even greater variety".[99] In 2012, it was awarded album of the year by *fRoots*, the publication that essentially brought about the reunion, and at the BBC Folk Awards, which also named June & Oysterband the band of the year, "Bonny Bunch Of Roses" traditional song of the year and June folk singer of the year, the second time she was accorded the honour, having won it eight years previously.

In her acceptance speech before the great and the good of British folk music at Manchester's Lowry Theatre, she name-checked Oysterband, Andy Cutting, Martin Simpson, Huw Warren, Mark Emerson and Tim Harries, all of whom were part of a collective that "have enabled me not just to use my voice, but my mind and my heart in sharing the songs that I love most, with you." June joked that she was "too damn lazy to play an instrument. I won't practice and the left hand knows not what the right is doing. So I just sing."[100]

The success of *Ragged Kingdom* has whet Ian Telfer's appetite for a third studio outing for June and Oysterband at some stage in the future – though a 21-year gap may not be advisable, given both parties' advancing years.

"I would very much like to do some more. One of the great things about June is she never stops thinking about songs. If we were to mentally schedule such a thing, I'm sure she'd come up with really good suggestions before we'd even start thinking about it. There's nothing planned yet. I think Topic Records would be clearly interested in such a thing. You have to mesh two timetables and two sets of plans. She's already done an album since *Ragged Kingdom*, and we've done another album. And anyway, it would be nice to leave it long enough so that it would be a slight surprise again."

That June can remain so relevant, so vital, after all this time, marks her out as among the most significant and progressive voices not only of her generation, but of Britain – or perhaps more appositely, of England – over the past five decades.

"A lot of people in the '70s and '80s in the folk scene, got very into technique," says Ian Telfer. "And June's technically a very, very accomplished singer, the vocal ornament and so forth. She loves a traditional song called 'Riding Down To Portsmouth', in which I think, she, tongue in cheek, put every possible piece of ornamentation and cleverness which she could think of into the vocal take, and it sounds to me very funny. To somebody who doesn't know where that take on the song is coming from, it probably sounds insane. But it was meant as humour. So she could do all that standing on her head. Like most people who were learning their chops in folk music in that period, she simplified her singing a lot – so has Martin Carthy, so have plenty of other people."

Despite such handsome plaudits, June believes she's still looking for her voice. "It changes. Over far too many years it's altered. The voice is going down. I obviously absorb certain things from other kinds of singing – not deliberately – and it keeps getting pared down and simplified. The art of timing of when and how you deliver a line is something you only acquire with age. That's as much singing technique as hitting the notes right. I used to use quite a lot of ornamentation and now I use virtually none. It's all down to timing.

"It's like any artistic activity. You learn the basics – the mechanics – of how to do something, and then you see what you can do with it, what you want to apply to it. In the end – and this is just something you come to eventually – the songs just really tell you how they want to be sung. Some people never get that far. It doesn't make them bad singers. For me, eventually it all came down to the words. I am a conduit."

She may have simplified her singing, but still June continues to go way beyond the folk landscape in which she was conceived as a singer, and immerse herself deeper in song, to plumb the fathoms of its mystery. She went still further with Quercus, which translates as oak in Latin, a trio also featuring Huw Warren and jazz saxophonist Iain Ballamy (augmented by Tim Harries on bass and drummer Martin France), who released a critically-lauded self-titled album in 2013.

Warren explains: "It was Iain's idea, but it arose from a couple of festivals – the Berlin Jazz Festival and the Kalisz Piano festival –

where the organisers were interested in both my projects and June. The logical compromise was to form an ensemble that could play my music and play with June. We wanted to create one sound rather than make crossovers. The original concept was to present June's songs alongside original music by myself and Iain, which I think has now developed into a concept of telling stories – whether it's with words or music."

It represents another departure from June's solid folk background, yet is threaded with folk elements. "Folk music has immeasurably enhanced my life and continues to do so, because of the wealth of great songs and stories," says June.

"The best of traditional music is timeless and totally relevant to every age through which it's passed, it really is. Equally, modern songwriting which is not pop, has huge relevance too. I was just wandering about in the garden this morning and I found myself singing Alistair Hulett's 'He Fades Away', which is an extraordinary song about loss and coping with the dreadful prospect of watching someone slowly dying in front of you because of the greed of people. Songs like that, songs like Bill Caddick's 'Unicorns' , the great narrative ballads, the love lyrics of the traditional, I can't imagine my life without them. I really can't."

Fourteen

A Fireball Of Emotion

♪

Teddy Thompson would like to dispel a myth. He wasn't responsible for resurrecting his mother's career by coaxing her back into the studio in 2002, after seventeen years away. "That seems to be the tag line," he says, "but she wanted to do it again."

Since 1985, Linda has enjoyed a happy marriage to Steve Kenis and derived maternal gratification from helping to navigate the safe passage into adulthood of her three children, Muna, Teddy and Kamila. There is pride too in Teddy's flowering as a singer-songwriter. And a truce had been declared between herself and Richard, possibly maintained by the "long distant" status of their relationship. The dysphonia continued to plague her but couldn't prevent her from returning to where she belonged, surrounded by musicians and singing her heart out.

"She was always singing around the house and always listening to music," Teddy remembers of that time. "When I think of lots of music that I heard in my pre-teens and early teens, when I was getting into music and records that stuck with me, they were coming from her. She was playing them in the car or singing them around the house."

Five of the ten songs on 2002's *Fashionably Late* were co-written by mother and son while one of the other five, "Paint & Powder Beauty", was a collaboration with Rufus Wainwright, the precocious offspring of Loudon Wainwright III and Kate McGarrigle.

"I didn't know Linda as a child. I may have met her when I was extremely young, but my mother and father definitely hung out with them a lot in the '70s in England. I was brought up in Canada, so

A Fireball Of Emotion

I don't think Canada was really on Linda's radar. She was pretty glamorous!" recalls Wainwright. "But when I really first came into contact with her was when I moved to Los Angeles, and I'd been signed by Dreamworks Records. Teddy Thompson was living there. He was a bit younger than me. All of a sudden Linda's antennae went up and she knew that I was going to California, and the whole back story, and she really kind of pushed for Teddy and I to spend some together. We then became very, very close friends – I became kind of the gay older brother! In fact, there's a famous story where we were hanging out a lot in Hollywood, and Teddy called Linda and said, 'Mom, everybody thinks I'm Rufus' boyfriend', and Linda said, 'Good!'

"I would see her in London. And when it really, really got close was when my mother was diagnosed with cancer, and Linda just became such a support to us on so many levels, whether it was professionally, singing for some of the benefits or the Christmas shows, or even when (sister) Martha had her son, Archangelo, prematurely, in London, Kate went and stayed with Linda in order to meet her grandchild, and Kate was very, very sick. Linda's sort of like our English guardian angel."

Wainwright believes Linda and his mother shared many similar traits, a commonality that cemented their enduring friendship. "I think they were both definite matriarchs – matriarchal powerhouses. They also were extremely talented and extremely in love with their husbands at certain points! I think both of them experienced very dramatic romantic lives with their folk singing husbands. And though it was painful and sad that it didn't work out, it was sort of a destiny that they had to fulfil and pass on to their children."

He was "very excited" to work with Linda on "Paint & Powder Beauty". She never once made him feel like the young buck he then was. "The way that she treats other musicians whom she respects is ageless. That's one of the fun facts about her – she'll just easily hang out with a Pete Seeger type or an Eminem type, as long as they kind of tickle her musical sensibilities.

"She's very, very generous. I wouldn't say she's a battleaxe in terms of going out there and working all the time. She's had her fair share of personal issues with her voice and so forth, so she's had to really contend with that. But when that is in a safe place, she's completely magnanimous.

"She's very beautiful – is very beautiful still. But when she was a young woman she was one of the great statuesque figures of the folk rock world. But her children just continue that tradition. I don't think I've ever met a woman with that many beautiful children, all of them. And when I met them they were all very much in London and living in Chelsea and having glamorous excursions, whereas I was stuck in freezing Canada. But I found that in a way growing up in the limelight has a price as well. It was sort of about that phenomenon. On the one hand I was impressed by the big time, but the older I get the happier I am that I was brought up in the cold north."

Richard and Kamila both feature on *Fashionably Late*, alongside a stellar cast, including Van Dyke Parks, Martin and Eliza Carthy, Kathryn Tickell and Geraint Watkins. It's hard to argue with *Rolling Stone's* assessment of it as "a long overdue gem from one of rock'n'roll's finest voices" and a "record of magnificent anguish". [101]

Teddy reckons it was his nascent career that got Linda "interested again in making music".

He explains, "I started writing quite late – properly in my early twenties. Then I started making records and had a bit of a career starting. My mum and I are very close – she was the person I would call when anything did happen. She was invested in what was going on with me musically. She was hearing a lot coming from me, and it obviously meant a lot to her because I'm her son, and it sort of got her juices flowing a bit again.

"I think she'd always been writing a bit, mostly lyrics – she strums the guitar, but she's not much of a player, really. I think she'd been jotting things down for a while, but about that time – which would be fifteen years ago – she started putting them together and thinking a bit more about writing more songs. And because she doesn't really play an instrument, she has a lot of lyrics but no tunes. And so basically that's how it started. I helped her write some tunes to her lyrics. She did do a bit of writing when she was with my dad. But it was a case that she was a novice writer and my dad was really good at it. So he tended to just blaze through things, so she didn't have a chance to contribute too much apart from here and there.

"Because we were living far away from each other, it was all via email. We wrote a little bit in the same room here and there when we were tightening things up, but not really. It's the best way for us to work. She can send me lots of ideas and lots of lyrics, and then I can take my time and see if anything comes to mind, and not have the pressure of your mum standing over you! That's a bit of a weird dynamic, especially when some of the songs are love songs. So we found a good working relationship in that sense."

Ed Haber is credited as producer on *Fashionably Late*, and it's he whom Teddy suggests did most to facilitate Linda's rebirth. "He started out as a fan. They're very comfortable together. He was the one that worked with her, and still works with her on her records. If it hadn't been for Ed being who he is... He's a very patient guy, willing to just try things, and if nothing happens, that's fine. So I think he deserves credit. If it had been anybody else, after a few sessions where they weren't getting anything, or if she was having trouble singing, they would go, 'I haven't got time for this'. But Ed really stuck with it and had the patience. Getting back to it was quite difficult after so many years."

You wait seventeen years for a second Linda Thompson album – and then you have to wait five more years for another. Not that she was idle during the interim, contributing "Je Veux Plus Te Voir" and "Valse De Balfa" – en Française – to *Evangeline Made: A Tribute To Cajun Music*, an album co-ordinated and produced by Ann Savoy.

"Since I am a huge fan of hers, I had hoped I could get her to sing some of our tragic Cajun songs. She speaks French. She nailed them, of course. I think Linda has the voice of a real woman, not a little girl. There is a depth and richness that is very adult and deep, what I consider a beautiful voice in a woman," says Savoy. "I was totally intimidated by her beauty and by what I know to be her talent, but she was really warm and funny, and maybe a little cynical, and very aware of all the people around her and appreciative of the people around her – not insular or snobbish, totally wonderful."

There was also the occasional family concert, Christmas shows with the McGarrigles and an appearance at Hal Wilner's Leonard Cohen tribute concerts, *Came So Far For Beauty*, where Linda performed "A Thousand Kisses Deep" and "Alexandra Leaving".

It was here that she met a young Anglo-American by the name of Antony Hegarty, who, in 2005, would win the UK's Mercury Music Prize for *I Am A Bird Now*, his debut album as the fulcrum of Antony And The Johnsons.

"I was star struck, as I have been a fan of her records," he tells me of that first encounter. "She was so kind to me, it touched me. We share a sense of humour. She can be quite irreverent, with a sense of humour as great as her humility. I fell in love with her, and when she asked me to sing on *Versatile Heart*, it was a no-brainer."

Versatile Heart, released in 2007, was, like *Fashionably Late*, also primarily a compositional two-hander with Teddy, though a standout track was Rufus Wainwright's "Beauty", written for Linda and sang as a duet by her and Hegarty, who enthuses, "We delivered it. It is a pleasure to sing with her. Later, we hung out with Liz Fraser (of Cocteau Twins) together, and I felt like I was witness to a great summit between two very great and humble singers."

The gap to Linda's next collection was longer still. But when it was eventually issued in 2013, *Won't Be Long Now* met with universal critical approval. Robin Denselow in *The Guardian* declared that she was "on remarkably powerful, confident form" and was "still compelling",[102] while according to Jim Wirth at *Uncut* magazine, the "folk rock grande dame" was "still damned grand".[103]

It's arguably her apotheosis – at least so far – as a writer, with the bleak shanty, "Never Put to Sea Boys", and "Love's For Babies And Fools" (written for Rufus Wainwright and enhanced by Richard's gaunt guitar) among the best things she's ever done.

"I was greatly moved," says Wainwright of the track. "I know she wants me to sing it at some point, and I'll definitely take her up on that offer. I like how it's a little spicy too. It's not an easy song. There's parts of me in there. I definitely put on quite a front when I began in the business. But like many in that case, that just means you're insecure. So I had to have very strong and brilliant armour."

Teddy insists that his contribution to *Won't Be Long Now* was minimal. "But what I did contribute was in that fashion, sending things back and forth. In the time between *Fashionably Late* and *Won't Be Long Now*, she's written more complete things. When she's asked for a contribution, it's been something smaller – help with a bridge or something – because she's gotten better at writing, I guess.

"The best attribute for a writer is to be honest. She's very honest. That's top of the list – you've got to tell the truth, otherwise it's not going to ring true. Her personality is that way. She's very straightforward and doesn't mince her words. She's got that going for her, she's good at that. She's a very good collaborator. It's not just me – there's a lot of collaboration on all of her recent records. And I think that's part of the product of her wanting help, because she still doesn't write a lot of songs from start to finish. She has bits and bobs of ideas. I think she's always looking for co-writers and people to help her. Co-writing is not an easy thing to do for most people. I don't do it with anybody else. She's very magnanimous and willing to accept other people's ideas. That's quite a skill, being able to do that."

For Linda, working with Teddy "is key. He writes with me and for me. He keeps my schmaltz in check. Old people are horribly sentimental. He's a great musician. We do clash a bit – he works fast, I work slow. I can't tell him what to do, like I can with other musos."

Won't Be Long Now also finds Linda co-writing with Ron Sexsmith on "If I Were A Bluebird". The Canadian one-man Lennon-McCartney did his bit by email. "It was really fun and easy. She sent me the lyrics and I wrote the music I think in a day or so. We wrote another one as well that I really liked, but I guess it didn't make it on the disc."

Quite when Linda's fifth album will come around, we just don't know. But we can hold on for it, if hold on we must, because she's earned the right to take however long she needs, and besides, she deserves our patience. For Linda Thompson has, like Maddy Prior and June Tabor, achieved a sense of pre-eminence. Teddy is justifiably proud and probably speaking for the rest of us when he says, "I think my mum really is a great singer, and I would use the word 'great'. It sounds so hackneyed, but there's a well of emotion which most people don't get to. I don't know how some people can access it, or how some people, when they open their mouths, you feel it, you know that it's true and you feel their pain, I suppose. But she's really got it.

"When she was young, when I listen to the old records, she had a very pure voice. She could do all the tricks if she wanted to, vocally, but she still had that very raw emotion. But now that she's 65, her voice has changed a lot and she's had problems singing, it's almost better in a way. Every syllable she utters... She's really walking a tightrope in some ways. She's kind of barely holding it together. She could break down and cry at any time. Like Ray Charles at the end of his life, for example, couldn't sing the way he used to. But all he had to do was moan and he would cut you to the quick. At this point in her life her voice is not as pure as it once was, but now added to it is a lifetime of experience and it's very moving. Some people just have it. She had it at the beginning, and in many ways she's gotten better as she's gotten older."

For Wainwright, Linda possesses "a tightrope of a voice". Every art form thrives on the idea of conflict, whether that conflict is made explicit within the art itself, or secreted within the heart and mind of the artist – there exists a sort of aesthetic tension between the art and the artist, between the real and the imagined. To truly convince as a singer is to acknowledge this tension, to confront it and resolve it, to release it in such a way the listener can realise it, can relate to it at some level

"Whether she likes it or not, she has to kind of latch on to a fireball of emotion," says Wainwright. "Sometimes it's a joyous, beautiful smooth ride, and other times it's a vicious rollercoaster. But in any case she never dials it in. And there's something thrilling about that.

There is a certain vulnerability and certain kind of delicate steel quality to it. I appreciate that. I really think it's fabulous how she keeps doing it, keeps making records and keeps putting herself out there. I really admire that."

Joe Boyd suggests that Linda's vocal problems "have limited her to a kind of Shirley Collins-like status – a legend that people will talk about having heard once live, and would love to hear again. When she's in good voice, she's one of the greats."

Despite the debilitating effects of her dysphonia, Linda shows no sign of slowing down. There are plans for a collaboration with Ann Savoy and Patty Griffin, and an album featuring the whole Thompson clan was released in November 2014.

Of the former, Savoy explains: "We are doing a follow-up to the CD I did with Linda Ronstadt called *Adieu False Heart*. I loved making a CD with Linda so much, and was so sad when she couldn't, because of her Parkinson's disease, do volume two. So I decided to find other women with amazing voices to do a duet with me. We also had the thought that we would do songs from our roots, so Linda will come with some Scottish songs, Patty some Acadian songs, me some Virginian songs. Who knows where it will all lead?"

The Thompson family album, *Family*, meanwhile proves that the family that doesn't stay together can still play together. Teddy, produced, having "cracked the whip with us all," according to Linda. Reviewing for the *Daily Telegraph*, Martin Chilton said: "It's a fine album – and well done the conciliatory middle son for bringing the family together. Well, musically, at least." [104]

The Guardian's Michael Hann, took a similar tone: "Goodness knows you wouldn't want to share a group therapy session with them, but it makes for a musically fabulous and lyrically compelling album."[105]

Linda says: "Me and Richard, we'd never have come up with this. We'd never have done it. But if your child asks you to do something, you're going to do it. I think it's more from the younger generation. Kami and Teddy wanted to do it and we wouldn't say no. We're not a very competitive family, but suddenly it's come in a bit. You don't want to be the worst on the record!"[106]

— Fifteen —

Essential Listening

¶

Such is the wealth of material released by Maddy, June and Linda since the 1960s, it would be impossible to critically appraise it all here. That's a whole other book. So I have, in a wholly subjective selection, identified some of those albums by each that are essential listening in terms of how they have evolved as singers – albums that arguably reflect the metamorphosis of British folk music following the second revival of the 1960s.

Tim Hart & Maddy Prior – Heydays (Folk Songs of Olde England Vol. 1, Folk Songs of Olde England Vol. 2, Summer Solstice)

Maddy's three albums with Tim Hart – all of which are compiled on 2003's *Heydays* – represent folk music at its most authentic. Ewan MacColl would have approved of the unalloyed renditions of "Lish Young Buy-A-Broom" and "The Dalesman's Litany" on *Folk Songs... Vol 1* particularly. Hart's minimal accompaniment on guitar, fiddle and banjo, and his subtle harmonies, allow Maddy's voice – young but impressively assured – to go deep into the songs. This first volume was recorded on mono over three days by Tee Pee Records head Tony Pike in the front room of his house at Dryburgh Road, Putney. "The photo session took longer than the album!"[107] quipped Hart.

Recording of the second volume was, compared to its predecessor, hi-tech as Pike opted for stereo, using a brace of Revox machines. Despite the enhanced sound – and Maddy playing a five-string banjo – the formula remains the same. Again, it's all about the material, including the first vinyl appearance of Grimsby songwriter

142

John Connolly's "Fiddler's Green", based on a mythical afterlife where there is perpetual mirth, a fiddle that never stops playing and dancers who never tire (which, when you think about it, sounds a whole lot like the folk scene), and "Copshawholme Fair', later appropriated by Steeleye Span.

It was when they were working on Steeleye Span's *Please To See The King* that Hart and Maddy completed their trilogy of albums as a duo. *Summer Solstice* was produced by Sandy Robertson and featured guest musicians Andy Irvine (mandolin), Gerry Conway (percussion and bells) and Pat Donaldson (electric bass), and a string arrangement by Robert Kirby on the devastating "Dancing At Whitsun", which laments the loss of so many young Englishmen in the First World War. This is one of two tracks anchored by Hart's vocal, the other being "The Ploughboy And The Cockney", though once more this collection is mainly about Maddy, superlative on "False Knight On The Road', "I Live Not Where I Love" and "Serving Girls Holiday".

One critic claimed that *Summer Solstice* was an exploitation of what constituted traditional folk song, a claim Hart eloquently refuted: "Traditional songs are living things. (Percy) Grainger collected in 1900-whatever, and he said anything collected then was traditional and anything done after ceased to be traditional. But traditional is any point in a song's career. We are ignoring that point in time developing them in relationship to contemporary musical forms. What's normally thought of as traditional is an artificial stopping in the life of a song. You can't say which way it's going to go, just as no-one can say what's going to be considered a traditional song in 200 years' time. Songs like these will outlive our great-grandchildren – they've already lasted several centuries."[108]

Steeleye Span – Hark! The Village Wait

Call me old-fashioned, but for my money *Hark! The Village Wait*, the only album by Steeleye Span's first line-up of Maddy, Tim Hart, Terry and Gay Woods, and Ashley Hutchings, stands alone as the definitive realisation of this electric folk institution's original blueprint – put crudely, to copulate past and present, and produce some kind of hybrid sonic progeny, something neither beautiful nor ugly, but ugly beautiful. The album is a guileless convergence of the traditional and the contemporary before the concept – and the band – became bloated on the bingeing excesses, both lyrical and musical, that came with bigger budgets, bigger studio and bigger egos in the 1970s especially. *Hark!...* manages to sound rough and regal, gritty and glorious, not unlike the Velvet Underground & Nico's eponymously-titled debut. Yes, Hutchings' bass is sometimes too loud and jarring, and the production occasionally ragged, but who cares? The point is it works.

Given the tension that simmered during rehearsals in Wiltshire, and later boiled over during the recording sessions at Sound Techniques Studio in London, it's plausible to suggest that the conflicting impressions engendered by listening to *Hark!...* are inevitable. Make no mistake, this is an edgy collection, loaded with punk attitude before punk had a name. The warring couples – Maddy and Hart, the Woods – "parted on fighting terms".[109] According to Hutchings, "By the time we'd finished the album, it was fully understood that we didn't want to meet again."[110]

Which is a bloody shame, really, not just because *Hark!...* has some compelling performances – "A Calling-On Song", "The Lowlands Of Holland", the concertina-led "The Dark-Eyed Sailor" and a lovely two-hander featuring Maddy and Gay Woods on "The Blacksmith", for example – but because it emphasises the very potent Irish blood that courses through the veins of British folk music. It's no coincidence that Terry Woods would go on to become an integral part of another Anglo-Irish outfit, The Pogues.

Sandy Robertson identified "the unique style or sound" that each of the players brought to the album. This, he said, combined with some great singers and songs, was what made *Hark!* ... appear "so fresh at the time".[111]

More than 40 years on, it still sounds fresh.

Steeleye Span – A Parcel Of Rogues

Steeleye Span's fifth album, *A Parcel Of Rogues*, was effectively the third incarnation of Ashley Hutchings' conception. Amid the fall-out from *Hark! The Village Wait*, Gay and Terry Woods left and were replaced by Martin Carthy and Peter Knight. Carthy stayed for a couple of albums only to quit (along with Hutchings) after *Ten Man Mop, Or Mr Reservoir Butler Rides Again*. Bob Johnson and Rick Kemp came in on guitar and bass and drums respectively, introducing a greater rock element. Maddy's delivery, though more strident as a consequence of everything being turned up in the mix, retains a folk sensibility, especially on "The Ups And Downs" and the Robert Burns poem, "Rogues In A Nation".

The overdubbing that became over-indulgent on later Steeleye Span albums is relatively restrained here, and indeed deployed discerningly, as in the triple channelling of Maddy's voice on "The Weaver And The Factory Maid". This song encapsulates the album's narrative principal theme – the struggle between old and new – in its depiction of early industrialisation, as a young man lauds the abundance of women in the factory, while a senior colleague recognises the inherent economic effects the same factory will wreak on the local community. The struggle is further articulated in the music, the trad. fiddle contrasting with Johnson's fretboard histrionics on "The Weaver And The Factory Maid", and the acoustic-drenched "The Ups And Downs" counterpointed by the distorted funk of "Robbery With Violins". It was a struggle in which the new emerged triumphant, as Steeleye Span added a second drummer, Nigel Pegrum, and embarked on a US tour in support of Jethro Tull, a period when Maddy made like a folk rock goddess before bemused audiences.

Steeleye Span – All Around My Hat

All Around My Hat makes the cut not just because it was Steeleye Span's commercial zenith, but because, with Mike Batt helming production, it steers electric folk – or folk rock, if you prefer (unlike certain others, I refuse to make a distinction between the two, as they're both predicated on the amplification of the acoustic) – into pop territory with considerable elan. Mike Batt mentioned in the same sentence as elan – who'd have thought it? Maddy's in exuberant form on the title track. The woman loves to sing and she clearly loves singing this song, which has, for good or ill, become her and Steeleye Span's signature. "Black Jack Davey" and "Hard Times Of Old England" aren't bad either.

Maddy Prior – Woman In The Wings

According to John Tobler, in the sleeve notes for *Woman In The Wings*, Maddy's 1978 solo debut may have been prompted by her sense that "the writing was on the wall"[112] for Steeleye Span. Such speculation is certainly plausible, given how precarious the situation was within the band at the time. She could have been making contingency plans – though I prefer to think she just wanted to develop an individual identity outside of the collective. Nothing wrong with that. Maddy enlisted the help of Jethro Tull's Ian Anderson as co-producer, while the entire Tull line-up appears at various stages, Martin Barre contributing a guitar solo on "Cold Flame", David Palmer (also listed as co-producer, along with engineer Robin Black) playing keyboards on the title track and "Mother And Child", and Anderson himself adorning "Gutter Geese" with his trademark flute.

Maddy is audibly trying to find herself, trying to establish her own voice away from Steeleye Span. She can't seem to make up her mind, and so she gads about the soundscapes, flirting with pop, rock and even jazz-lite ("I Told You So", "Baggy Pants"), and rushing back to the folk familiar. It's a bit like a first novel in that occasionally there's too much going on, too many influences in the mix, but it's impossibly beguiling for all that.

What really impresses is Maddy's writing – nothing is wasted. There's a poetic discipline to the lingual rhythm, particularly on the already mentioned "Mother And Child" and "Gutter Geese". And, of course, it's very tempting to hear both "Woman In The Wings" itself and "Rollercoaster" as autobiography.

Maddy Prior – Ravenchild

Apparently inspired by a TV wildlife series, much of *Ravenchild* explores the myths surrounding ravens, regarded by Europeans as birds of bad omen and associated with death, and tricksters or creators to Native Americans. And so we get compositions about juvenile ravens ("Young Bloods") fleeing the nest – literally – and gathering in gangs to feast on feeding grounds scavenging ravens ("Rich Pickings") and lovestruck ravens ("Ravenchild"). It could, and perhaps should, be mind-numbingly mundane, but Maddy's own fascination with the concept suffuses her vocals with a rich emotional depth, while the ethereal production by Nick Holland and the ridiculously versatile Troy Donockley (who also plays uilleann pipes, electric and acoustic guitars, low and tin whistles and cittern) transforms the melodic accompaniment into a potently evocative whole. Sure, the refined rap on "Rich Pickings" sounds a little incongruous, but you've got to admire Maddy's *chutzpah* in daring to be hip. Before the suite of songs about ravens, there's a neo-Napoleonic set bountiful of inspired arrangements (again, credit here must go to Messrs Holland and Donockley), a rousing rhythm-heavy "Twankydillo", the heartbreaking "Bold Poachers" (performed by Tim Hart on Steeleye Span's *A Parcel Of Rogues*) and biting social commentary of "Rigs Of The Time", on which Maddy lacerates multinational companies (the "unaccountable, faceless ones"), private utilities and the "media circus".

Maddy Prior – Seven For Old England

Maddy goes back to her folk roots on this collection to cover songs that span not just the years but the centuries. She took herself off to the Vaughan Williams Memorial Library at Cecil Sharp House to dig out the material, the majority of which she had never sung before but which was familiar to her from the folk club circuit and fellow performers. Benji Kirkpatrick and Giles Lewin form the musical fulcrum, with occasional contributions from Barney Morse-Brown, Tony Poole, John Banks and John Kirkpatrick, presenting "these jewels in the simplest, acoustic formats, leaving the songs to reveal their power quietly".[113] Maddy's voice has seldom sounded better than on "Dives And Lazarus" (with a melody appropriated from "The Star Of The County Down"), "Trooper's Nag" and "In Sad And Ashy Weeds", consummate exemplars in the art of interpretation.

Maddy Prior with The Carnival Band – A Tapestry Of Carols

Any of the nine albums Maddy has done with The Carnival Band could have been included here – it just so happens that *A Tapestry Of Carols* was their first collaboration. A collection of ancient carols from across Europe, it demonstrates the breadth of Maddy's redoubtable facility as a singer. This is not easy music for someone technically unschooled in music to tackle, but then Maddy Prior has never shied away from a challenge. The process was made more comfortable for her by the deliberate decision on the part of everyone concerned to "shut out all memories of cathedral choirs, brass bands and supermarket jingles. We took the tunes and words just as we would any other song and allowed them to dictate the style, speed, harmonies and instrumentation."[114] The results are quite remarkable, not least on "Angels From The Realms Of Glory".

Maddy Prior with Hannah James & Giles Lewin – 3 For Joy

She may be in her sixties, but Maddy continues to push forward instead of looking back. She has worked with Giles Lewin (as a member of The Carnival Band) since 1991. On *3 For Joy*, a beautiful magpie of an album, they are joined by singer, accordionist and clog dancer Hannah James, one of the next generation of British folk artists. She brings some interesting ethno-music ideas to the project, including "Nauchila Sa Hubava Doina", and, together with Lewin, enhances Maddy's lead with perfectly judged harmonies, especially on "Dacre". You can only hazard a guess as to which musical direction Maddy pursues next, but one thing's for certain – it won't be predictable.

A very young Richard and Linda Thompson.
(*Unknown photographer. Image courtesy of Linda Thompson*)

The quality of these photographs may not be great, but they are unique.
We are so grateful to Linda for letting us include these very
rare pictures from her own collection.
(*Unknown photographers. Images courtesy of Linda Thompson*)

Actor Peter O'Toole presents Linda with Best Original Song for "No Telling" at the Radio 2 Folk Awards in 2003. The two were close friends. (*Photo by Richard Young/Rex*)

Linda with son Teddy and Rufus Wainwright (centre) at a party in the Dorchester Hotel, London, 2007. Rufus describes Linda as an "English Guardian Angel". (*Photo by Richard Young/Rex*)

Linda demonstrates what fun it is to play the ukulele.
(*Photographer unknown. Image courtesy of Linda Thompson*)

Maddy Prior & June Tabor – Silly Sisters

Maddy was in her pomp with Steeleye Span when Chrysalis mooted the idea of a project away from the band. She and friend June Tabor had flirted with harmonies at the Bromyard Festival in 1973. They sounded good together. Immortalising their vocal relationship on record was only a matter of time. *Silly Sisters* became not only the first of two albums Maddy and June recorded together, but the name by which they became known as a duo. It digs into both women's folk roots on a selection of songs ranging from the Child ballads, "Burning Of Auchindoon" and "Lass Of Loch Royal", through "Singing The Travels" (collected from the Symondsbury Mummers) and The Copper Family's "Dame Durden", to Cyril Tawney's autobiographical "The Grey Funnel Line", about the daily drudgery experienced by a sailor in the Royal Navy, punctuated by the transient joy of homecoming and the poignant sadness of leaving again. Maddy and June's voices interlace, they soar and they swoop, they get deep into character, whether that character is a doffer charged with changing the bobbins on the weaving looms in "Doffin' Mistress", or the sexually frustrated wife whose husband can't get it up on "My Husband's Got No Courage". There's beauty, profundity and comedy here, all of it delivered by two singers in perfect symmetry and aided by a crack collective of musicians including Martin Carthy, Nic Jones, Andy Irvine, Johnny Moynihan and Danny Thompson.

Silly Sisters: Maddy Prior & June Tabor – No More To The Dance

Ten years after their first collaboration, Maddy and June reunited for *No More To The Dance*. It's less traditional than its predecessor but no less captivating for that. You can hear how confident June has become as a vocalist during the gap between both albums, especially on "Rosie Anderson" (performed alone with just Huw Warren for accompaniment on piano), which presaged the minimalist direction her solo career would subsequently take. Maddy too gets her own spot on Rick Kemp's "Somewhere Along The Road", but of course it's the pair of them you want to hear together on the likes of "Fine Horseman" and "How Shall I Your True Love Know?" Musically, *No More To The Dance* is sumptuously arranged around Warren's keys and Dan Ar Bras' guitar. We're still waiting for the third instalment of Silly Sisters.

June Tabor – Airs And Graces

Yes, it's mostly about June's definitive reading of Eric Bogle's anti-war narrative, "The Band Played Waltzing Matilda" – powerful sentiments conveyed here *a cappella*, stark as the wasteland of Gallipoli after the last bodies have bled their sacrifice into the earth – but there's much more to enjoy on *Airs And Graces*, including 'Plains Of Waterloo' and "Reynardine", the Child ballads "Bonny May", "Young Waters" and "Waly Waly", and the channelling of Belle Stewart's spirit on "Queen Among The Heather". The accompaniment throughout is both frugal and judicious, with Nic Jones (guitar, fiddle), Tony Hall (melodeon) and Jon Gillaspie (piano, organ, roxichord, bassoon and sopranino) merely illuminating June's dark, dominant timbre with shafts of sonic colour.

June Tabor – Aqaba

June's return to recording after a five-year sabbatical, *Aqaba* was a transition between old and new accompanists, Martin Simpson and Huw Warren, and a compound of old and new material. The former includes another of June's superlative interpretations – this time it's Natalie Merchant's "Verdi Cries" – while among the latter, she affirms her place within the folk pantheon as the uncrowned queen of melancholy on "The Banks Of Red Roses" and the Yiddish dirge about the plight of sweatshop workers, "Mayn Rue Plats". The title track, penned by Bill Caddick, makes Lawrence of Arabia into flesh and blood as he confronts his mortality. A haunting, deeply affecting piece of work.

June Tabor And The Oyster Band – Freedom And Rain

June has always resisted the label of folk singer, preferring to see herself – remember Chapter Ten of this book? – as "a singer of songs that tell good stories. It doesn't matter where they come from." If there were any doubts that this was the case, June dispelled them on her first collaboration with The Oyster Band. The lion's share of tracks on *Freedom And Rain* are from the contemporary era and the pens of living writers such as Shane MacGowan ("Lullaby Of London"), Richard Thompson ("Night Comes In"), Billy Bragg ("Valentine's Day Is Over") and Lou Reed ("All Tomorrow's Parties"). There's a certain menace to June's icy take on Bragg in particular.

The traditional songs are fused with a rock energy and bulwarked by punk attitude, especially the irresistible, brass-heavy madness that is "Dives And Lazarus". For someone who had never fronted a band before – indeed someone who once found it daunting to sing with any kind of accompaniment – June's formidable chops are more than a match for The Oyster Band's rowdy racket.

June Tabor – An Echo Of Hooves

June, surrounded by her now regular pool of accompanists, Huw Warren (piano, cello, piano accordion), Mark Emerson (viola, violin, piano) and Tim Harries (double bass), is reunited with guitarist Martin Simpson for the first time since *Aqaba*. Northumbrian piper Kathryn Tickell rounds out the line-up, appropriate given that many of the traditional ballads that comprise *An Echo Of Hooves* originate from the English/Scottish border regions. The stark, uncompromising narratives (but when has June ever compromised her artistic sensibility?) pulsate with violence, whether on "Bonnie James Campbell", "The Battle Of Otterburn" or "The Border Widow's Lament". Not for the lily-livered.

June Tabor – Ashore

"A fascination with the sea has become part of my life, and even now I feel a genuine excitement when boarding a ferry, any ferry,

151

wherever it might be going,"[115] says June of her second concept album, *Ashore* (the first, a celebration of the rose, was 2001's *Rosa Mundi*). You won't hear any raucous sea shanties on this paean to the great oceans, but rather songs that "speak of the horrors of battle at sea, the misery, the vicious ill treatment and the powerlessness of the individual on board ship, as graphically as any film. Emigration, shipwreck, cannibalism, seemingly endless bitter weather and privation are all here." Cyril Tawney's "The Oggie Man", Ian Telfer's "Finisterre" and a rendition of Elvis Costello's "Shipbuilding" that is every bit the equal of Robert Wyatt's (and that's high praise), are among the pearls in this watery collection.

June Tabor & Oysterband – Ragged Kingdom

fRoots editor Ian Anderson deserves our gratitude for bringing about the eventual sequel to *Freedom And Rain* 21 years later. It was Anderson who, following a benefit concert for his publication at London's Roundhouse, suggested that June and the Oysters recorded another album. When it eventually arrived, *Ragged Kingdom* was so damn good, we almost forgot how long both parties had kept us waiting. Almost. *Ragged Kingdom* retains much of *Freedom And Rain*'s verve, as well as its adventurous spirit (a tender, aching remake of Joy Division's lugubrious "Love Will Tear Us Apart" is a duet between June and Oysterband's John Jones, for example, while there is a bold reworking of P.J. Harvey's "That Was My Veil" and a brilliantly intense "Bonny Bunch Of Roses"), added to which is a greater sense of sophistication and emotional acuity. Who knows when – and indeed if - they'll next work together in the studio? Perhaps now is an apposite time to drum up a petition...

Quercus – Quercus

Quercus is the Latin appellation (meaning 'oak') given to June, Huw Warren and Iain Ballamy, and to their debut album as a trio – a rootsy folk set with a jazz accent. On occasions the serenity and fragility at the heart of these songs – "As I Roved Out" and "Come Away Death", for example – is enough to still the breath in rapt attention, but there are moments too when both the gloom and the tempo are raised, such as on "Near But Far Away" and the tango that ignites "Who Wants the Evening Rose?" June's unaccompanied rendering of "Brigg Fair" is a potent reminder that she remains a solo singer without equal.

Richard and Linda Thompson – I Want To See The Bright Lights Tonight

Richard Thompson was never a folkie. Not really. The parameters of the music – and the culture that went with it – were way too restrictive for an artist with his creative ambition. Undeterred by the first faltering steps of his solo career post-Fairport Convention – namely the underwhelming response to his debut album, *Henry The Human Fly* – he found the perfect foil in Linda Peters-come-Thompson for songs that flitted between horrible, hard-boiled cynicism and gentle humanism. She's a revelation here. With a voice sculpted by angels, Linda eschews drama for a cooler, more measured delivery on "Withered And Died", "Down Where The Drunkards Roll" and "Has He Got A Friend For Me?' These are weighty narratives but she makes them work, a testament to her indomitable spirit as a singer.

Richard and Linda Thompson – Shoot Out The Lights

Probably the most acrimonious break-up album ever, although the break-up in this instance occurred a couple of years after Richard Thompson wrote the songs for his and Linda's final release – so, technically, not a break-up album at all. But when have the facts ever prevented fertile imaginations from generating convenient narratives? Given the bitter fall-out on the US tour to promote *Shoot Out The Lights*, it is, however, impossible not to place the album in the context of an imploding marriage. And so what if the songs were written when Richard and Linda were still together as husband and wife? Scan the lyrics of "Don't Renege On Our Love", "Walking On A Wire' or "A Man In Need" and the cracks were evident long before the tortuous denouement. Certainly Richard didn't appear to be a happy bunny – just listen to the venom in his vocal delivery and the barbed wire guitar he plays here. God knows how Linda manages to retain her equilibrium while knee deep in such emotional tumult. But she does, and in so doing earns our considerable respect. Of course, the consummate artist in the studio later mutated into the scorned missus on stage. It wasn't pretty but it was pardonable.

Linda Thompson – Fashionably Late

Seventeen years on from her previous solo effort – 1985's *One Clear Moment* – and seemingly recovered from the dysphonia that truncated her career, Linda's comeback was somewhat premature. It would be another five years before the next album, *Versatile Heart*, and six more years until *Won't Be Long Now*. By the time of *Fashionably Late*, she and Richard had brokered a peace – he features on "Dear Mary". But it's another Thompson male, son Teddy, whose dabs are all over this collection. He co-writes seven of the ten tracks and chips in on guitar and (with sister Kamila) on harmony vocals. The goodwill towards Linda, her popularity among her peers, is evidenced by the appearance of Van Dyke Parks, Martin Carthy, Dave Mattacks and Dave Pegg, while young folkies such as Kate Rusby, John McCusker, Eliza Carthy and Kathryn Tickell also lend their artistry to the project. Linda's in fine voice on an album that's mostly melancholy and mostly anchored in the tradition – with "Nine Stone Rig" and "The Banks Of The Clyde" particularly fine examples – though the jazz-inflected "Paint & Powder Beauty" (on which Rufus Wainwright shares a writing credit with Linda) is an exquisite Cole Porter impersonation.

Linda Thompson – Won't Be Long Now

"Life's short and getting shorter", sings Linda on the title track of *Won't Be Long Now*. The lyric was written for her by Teddy. "What's his point, I wonder?" she quips in the sleeve notes. Don't be misled by the above line, however – for "Won't Be Long Now", far from being a eulogy for his mother, is actually a cautionary tale. Linda sings in a ragged voice inhibited by her condition, but a ragged voice that continues to bewitch on an album that has finally liberated her from Richard's shadow and trumped anything else she's previously offered up as a solo artist, whether on "Love's For Babies And Fools" (about Rufus Wainwright), "If I Were A Bluebird" (co-written with Ron Sexsmith) or the traditional powerhouses, "Paddy's Lamentation" and "Blue Bleezin' Blind Drunk". We can only hope that Linda can stay healthy and that there's more where that came from, but if *Won't Be Long Now* is to be her swansong as a solo artist, it's a magisterial *adieu*.

Discographies

9

The following discographies document the studio recordings, live albums and compilations of Maddy Prior, June Tabor and Linda Thompson. The Steeleye Span discography documents studio recordings only on which Maddy appears. The various anthologies and other albums on which Maddy, June and Linda feature are not included, nor are June's collaborations with The Mrs Ackroyd Band or Linda's with The Home Service.

Tim Hart & Maddy Prior

Folk Songs Of Old England Vol. 1 (Tepee Records, UK, 1968)
Produced by Tony Pike.
Lish Young Buy-A-Broom/Adieu Sweet Lovely Nancy/Maid That's Deep In Love/The Rambling Sailor/Bruton Town/Farewell Nancy/The Dalesman's Litany/The Brisk Butcher/The Stately Southerner/Who's The Fool Now?/A Wager A Wager/Babes In The Wood/Adam And Eve

Folk Songs Of Old England Vol. 2 (Tepee Records, UK, 1969)
Produced by Tony Pike.
My Son John/Earl Richard/Paddy Stole The Rope/The Gardener/Bay Of Biscay/Queen Eleanor's Confession/Horn Of The Hunter/ Copshawholme Fair/Oats And Beans And Barley Grows/Fiddler's Green/ Captain Wedderburn's Courtship/Turkey Rhubarb/The Bold Fisherman

Summer Solstice (B & C Records, UK, 1971)
Produced by Sandy Robertson
Musicians: Andy Irvine (mandolin), John Ryan (string bass), Gerry Conway (percussion, bells), Pat Donaldson (electric bass), Robert Kirby (string arrangement on "Dancing At Whitsun").
False Knight On The Road/Bring Us In Good Ale/Of All the Birds/

I Live Not Where I Love/The Ploughboy And The Cockney/Westron Wynde/Sorry The Day I Was Married/Dancing At Whitsun/Fly Up My Cock/Cannily Cunnily/Adam Catched Eve/Three Drunken Maidens/ Serving Girls Holiday

Heydays: The Solo Recordings 1968-1976 (Castle Music, UK, 2003)
This compilation features all three albums, *Folk Songs Of Old England Vols 1* and *2*, and *Summer Solstice*.

Heritage (Disky Records, Netherlands, 2003)
This Dutch compilation features 16 tracks selected from *Folk Songs Of Old England Vols 1* and *2*.
The Rambling Sailor/Bruton Town/Farewell Nancy/The Brisk Butcher/ The Stately Southerner/Who's The Fool Now? /Babes In The Wood/ My Son John/Earl Richard/Horn Of The Hunter/Oats And Beans And Barley Grows/Fiddler's Green/Turkey Rhubarb/Copshawholme Fair/ The Bold Fisherman

Steeleye Span

Hark! The Village Wait (RCA, UK, 1970)
Produced by Sandy Robertson and Steeleye Span
Musicians: Maddy Prior (step dancing, five-string banjo), Tim Hart (vocals, electric guitar, five-string banjo, electric dulcimer, fiddle, harmonium), Ashley Hutchings (electric bass), Gay Woods (vocals, autoharp, concertina, bodhran, step dancing), Gerry Conway (drums), Dave Mattacks (drums)
A Calling-On Song/The Blacksmith/Fisherman's Wife/The Blackleg Miner/The Dark-Eyed Sailor/Copshawholme Fair/All Things Are Quite Silent/The Hills Of Greenmore/My Johnny Was A Shoemaker/ Lowlands Of Holland/Twa Corbies/One Night As I Lay On My Bed

Please To See The King (B & C, UK, 1971)
Produced by Sandy Robertson
Maddy Prior (vocals, spoon, tabor, tambourine, bells), Martin Carthy (vocals, guitar, banjo, organ, bells), Tim Hart (vocals, guitar, dulcimer,

bells), Ashley Hutchings (vocals, bass guitar, bells), Peter Knight (vocals, fiddle, mandolin, organ, bass guitar, bells)
The Blacksmith/Cold, Haily, Windy Night/Jigs: Bryan O'Lynn-The Hag With The Money/Prince Charlie Stuart/Boys Of Bedlam/False Knight On The Road/The Lark In The Morning/Female Drummer/The King/ Lovely On The Water

Ten Man Mop Or Mr Reservoir Butler Rides Again (Pegasus, UK, 1971)
Musicians: Maddy Prior (vocals, spoons, tabor), Tim Hart (vocals, dulcimer, guitars, organ, five-string banjo, mandolin), Peter Knight (vocals, fiddle, tenor banjo, mandolin, timpani), Martin Carthy (vocals, guitar, organ), Ashley Hutchings (bass)
Gower Wassail/Jigs: Paddy Clancy's Jig-Willie Clancy's Fancy/Four Nights Drunk/When I Was On Horseback/Marrowbones/Captain Coulston/Reels: Dowd's Favourite-£10 Float-The Morning Dew/ Wee Weaver/Skewball

Below The Salt (Chrysalis, 1972)
Produced by Steeleye Span and Jerry Boys
Musicians: Maddy Prior (vocals, tambourine), Tim Hart (vocals, guitar, acoustic guitar, dulcimer, tabor, spoons), Bob Johnson (vocals, guitar, acoustic guitar), Peter Knight (violin, viola, mandolin, tenor banjo, piano, vocals), Rick Kemp (bass, drums, vocals)
Spotted Cow/Rosebud In June/Jigs: The Bride's Favourite-Tansey's Fancy/Sheep Crook And Black Dog/Royal Forester/King Henry/ Gaudete/John Barleycorn/Saucy Sailor

Parcel Of Rogues (Chrysalis, UK, 1973)
Produced by Steeleye Span and Jerry Boys
Musicians: Maddy Prior (vocals), Tim Hart (guitar, dulcimer, vocals), Bob Johnson (guitar, vocals), Rick Kemp (bass, drums, vocals), Peter Knight (violin, viola, mandolin, piano, recorders, harmonium, vocals)
One Misty Moisty Morning/Alison Gross/The Bold Poachers/The Ups And Downs/Robbery With Violins/The Wee Wee Man/The Weaver And The Factory Maid/Rogues In A Nation/Cam Ye O'er Frae France/ Hares On The Mountain

Discographies

Now We Are Six (Chrysalis, UK, 1974)
Produced by Ian Anderson
Musicians: Maddy Prior (vocals), Tim Hart (acoustic guitar, vocals, electric dulcimer, banjo), Peter Knight (vocals, violin, acoustic guitar, piano, tenor banjo, mandolin), Robert Johnson (electric and acoustic guitar, vocals, synthesiser), Rick Kemp (bass, vocals), Nigel Pegrum (drums, recorder, oboe, flute, tambourine), The St Eleye Primary School Junior Choir (vocals), David Bowie (alto sax)
Seven Hundred Elves/Edwin/Drink Down The Moon-The Cuckoo/ Now We Are Six/Thomas The Rhymer/The Mooncoin Jig/Long-A-Growing/Two Magicians/Twinkle, Twinkle, Little Star/To Know Him Is To Love Him

Commoners Crown (Chrysalis, UK, 1975)
Produced by Steeleye Span and Robin Black
Musicians: Maddy Prior (vocals), Tim Hart (vocals, guitar, dulcimer), Robert Johnson (guitar, vocals), Rick Kemp (bass, vocals), Peter Knight (violin), Nigel Pegrum (drums, flute), Peter Sellers (acoustic ukulele)
Little Sir Hugh/Bach Goes To Limerick/Long Lankin/Dogs And Ferrets/Galtee Farmer/Demon Lover/Elf Call/Weary Cutters/ New York Girls

All Around My Hat (Chrysalis, UK, 1975)
Produced by Mike Batt
Musicians: Maddy Prior (vocals), Tim Hart (vocals, guitar, dulcimer), Bob Johnson (vocals, guitar), Rick Kemp (vocals, bass guitar), Peter Knight (vocals, violin, mandolin)
Black Jack Davy/Hard Times Of Old England/Cadgwith Anthem/ Sum Waves (Tunes)/The Wife Of Usher's Well/Gamble Gold-Robin Hood/All Around My Hat/Dance With Me/Bachelors Hall

Rocket Cottage (Chrysalis, UK, 1976)
Produced by Mike Batt
Musicians: Maddy Prior (vocals), Tim Hart (vocals, guitar), Bob Johnson (vocals, guitar), Rick Kemp (bass guitar, vocals), Peter Knight (violin, mandolin), Nigel Pegrum (drums)

London/The Bosnian Hornpipes/Orfeo-Nathan's Reel/The Twelve
Witches/The Brown Girl/Fighting For Strangers/Sligo Maid/
Sir James The Rose/The Drunkard

Storm Force Ten (Chrysalis, UK, 1977)
Produced by Steeleye Span and Mike Thompson
Musicians: Maddy Prior (vocals), John Kirkpatrick (vocals, accordion),
Martin Carthy (vocals, guitar), Rick Kemp (bass), Nigel Pegrum (drums)
Awake, Awake/Sweep, Chimney Sweep/The Wife Of The Soldier/
The Victory/The Black Freighter/Some Rival/Treadmill Song/
Seventeen Come Sunday

Live At Last! (Chrysalis, UK, 1978)
Recorded live at the Winter Gardens, Bournemouth
Engineered by Mike Thompson
Musicians: Maddy Prior (vocals), John Kirkpatrick (vocals, accordion),
Martin Carthy (vocals, guitar), Tim Hart (vocals, guitar), Rick Kemp
(bass), Nigel Pegrum (drums)
The Atholl Highlanders-Walter Bulwer's Polka/Saucy Sailor-Black
Freighter/The Maid And The Palmer/Hunting The Wren/Montrose/
Bonnets So Blue/The False Knight On The Road

Sails Of Silver (Chrysalis, UK, 1980)
Produced by Gus Dudgeon
Musicians: Maddy Prior (vocals), Tim Hart (vocals, guitar), Bob Johnson
(vocals, guitar), Rick Kemp (vocals, bass), Peter Knight (vocals, keyboards,
violin), Nigel Pegrum (drums, percussion, woodwind)
Sails Of Silver/My Love/Barnet Fair/Senior Service/Gone To America/
Where Are They Now?/Let Her Go Down/Longbone/
Marigold-Harvest Home/Tell Me Why

Back In Line (Flutterby, UK, 1986)
Produced by Steeleye Span and John Acock
Musicians: Maddy Prior (vocals), Peter Knight (violin, vocals),
Rick Kemp (bass, vocals), Bob Johnson (guitar, vocals), Nigel Pegrum
(drums), Vince Cross (Yamaha DX7 synthesiser)
Edward/Lanercost/Lady Diamond/Isabel/A Canon By Telemann/

Discographies

Blackleg Miner/Peace On The Border/Scarecrow/Take My Heart/
White Man

Tempted And Tried (Dover, UK, 1989)
Produced by John Etchells, Bob Johnson and Peter Knight
Musicians: Maddy Prior (lead vocals, backing vocals), Peter Knight
(violins, mandolin, backing vocals), Bob Johnson (guitars, lead vocals,
backing vocals), Nigel Pegrum (drums, percussion), Tim Harries (bass,
piano, backing vocals), Martin Ditchum (extra percussion)
Padstow/The Fox/Two Butchers/Following Me/Seagull/The Cruel
Mother/Jack Hall/Searching For Lambs/Shaking Of The Sheets/
Reels: The First House In Connaught-Sailor's Bonnet/Betsy Bell And
Mary Gray

Time (Park Records, UK, 1996)
Produced by Steeleye Span and John Etchells
Musicians: Maddy Prior (vocals), Gay Woods (vocals, bodhran),
Bob Johnson (vocals, electric guitar), Peter Knight (vocals, violin),
Tim Harries (bass, keyboards, vocals), Liam Genockey (drums,
percussion)
The Prickly Bush/The Old Maid In The Garret-Tam Lin/Harvest Of The
Moon/Underneath Her Apron/The Cutty Wren/Go From My Window/
The Elf-Knight/The Water Is Wide/You Will Burn/Corbies/
The Song Will Remain

They Called Her Babylon (Park Records, UK, 2004)
Produced by Steeleye Span
Musicians: Maddy Prior (vocals), Peter Knight (vocals, violin, Octave
violin, keyboards), Ken Nicol (vocals, guitars), Rick Kemp (vocals, bass),
Liam Genockey (drums)
Van Diemen's Land/Samain/Heir Of Linne/Bride's Farewell/They Called
Her Babylon (The Siege Of Lathom House)/Mantle Of Green/Bede's
Death Song/Diversus And Lazarus/Si Begh Si Mohr/Child Owlet/
What's The Life Of A Man?

Winter (Park Records, UK, 2004)
Produced by Steeleye Span

Musicians: Maddy Prior (vocals), Peter Knight (violin, Octave violin, viola, electric piano, mandolin, backing vocals, string arrangements), Ken Nicol (vocals, acoustic and electric guitars), Rick Kemp (bass, vocals), Liam Genockey (drums and percussion)
The First Nowell/Down In Yon Forest/Unconquered Sun/Chanticleer/ Bright Morning Star/Winter/See Amid The Winter's Snow/Mistletoe Bough/Sing We The Virgin Mary/Today In Bethlehem/Blow Your Trumpet Gabriel/Hark The Herald Angels Sing/Good King Wenceslas/ In The Bleak Midwinter

Bloody Men (Park Records, UK, 2006)
Produced by Steeleye Span
Musicians: Maddy Prior (vocals), Peter Knight (violin, vocals), Rick Kemp (bass, vocals), Ken Nicol (guitars, vocals), Liam Genockey (drums and percussion)
The Bonny Black Hare/The Story Of The Scullion King/The Dreamer And The Widow/Lord Elgin/The Three Sisters/The First House In Connaught-The Lady Of The House/Cold Haily Windy Night/ Whummil Bord/Demon Of The Well/Lord Gregory/Ned Ludd Part 1 (Inclosure)/Ned Ludd Part 2 (Rural Retreat)/Ned Ludd Part 3 (Ned Ludd)/Ned Ludd Part 4 (Prelude To Peterloo)/Ned Ludd Part 5 (Peterloo The Day)

Cogs, Wheels And Lovers (Park Records, UK, 2009)
Produced by Steeleye Span with Mark Ellis and Tony Poole
Musicians: Maddy Prior (vocals), Peter Knight (violin, vocals), Rick Kemp (bass, vocals), Ken Nicol (guitars, vocals), Liam Genockey (drums, percussion)
The Gallant Frigate Amphitrite/Locks and Bolts/Creeping Jane/Just As the Tide/Ranzo/The Machiner's Song/Our Captain Cried/Two Constant Lovers/Madam, Will You Walk/The Unquiet Grave/Thornaby Woods/ The Great Silkie Of Sule Skerry

Wintersmith (Park Records, UK, 2013)
Produced by Steeleye Span
Musicians: Maddy Prior (vocals), Peter Knight (violin, violins, piano), Rick Kemp (bass, vocals), Liam Genockey (drums, percussion), Julian Littman (guitar, vocals, piano), Pete Zorn (acoustic guitar,

saxophone, vocals), Terry Pratchett (vocals), Kathryn Tickell
(Northumbrian pipes), Bob Johnson (vocals), John Spiers (melodeon)
Overture: Ancient Eyes & The Dark Morris Tune/The Dark Morris
Song/Wintersmith/You/The Good Witch/Band Of Teachers/The Wee
Free Men/Hiver/Fire & Ice/The Making Of A Man/Crown & Ice/
First Dance/The Dark Morris Tune/The Summer Lady/Ancient Eyes/
We Shall Wear Midnight

Maddy Prior

Woman In The Wings (Chrysalis, UK, 1978)
Produced by Ian Anderson, David Palmer and Robin Black
Musicians: Maddy Prior (vocals), Andy Roberts (guitar), Barriemore
Barlow (drums), John Glascock (bass), David Palmer (keyboards),
David Olney (bass), Martin Barre (guitar) Barry Booth (piano),
Ian Anderson (flute), John Halsey (drums), Bob Gill (guitar), Shona
Anderson, Cherry Gillespie (backing vocals), Patrick Halling (leader of
strings), Don Morgan (leader of brass)
Woman In The Wings/Cold Flame/Mother And Child/Gutter Geese/
Rollercoaster/Deep Water/Long Shadows/I Told You So/Rosettes/
Catseyes/Baggy Pants

Changing Winds (Chrysalis, UK, 1978)
Produced by Davy Rohl
Musicians: Maddy Prior (vocals), Richie Close (Fender Rhodes,
Hammond C-3, piano, pianette), Chris Stainton, Sarah Deco (piano),
Doug Morter (lead guitar), John O'Connor (electric guitar, acoustic
guitar, classical guitar), Kevin Savigar (synthesiser, harpsichord), Rick
Kemp (bass), B.J. Cole (pedal steel guitar), David Hassell,
John Lingwood (percussion), Glyn Thomas (syndrums), Malcolm Peet
(bottleneck guitar), Philip Todd (saxophone, clarinet), Rick Kemp,
Doug Morter, John O'Connor, Barbara Dickson, Sara Deco (backing
vocals), Jack Rothstein (leader of strings)
To Have And To Hold/Pity The Poor Night Porter/Bloomers/
Accappella Stella/Canals/The Sovereign Prince/Ali Baba/The Mountain/
In Fighting/Another Drink

Hooked On Winning (Kempire, UK, 1982)
Produced by The Maddy Prior Band and Dave Cook
Musicians: Maddy Prior (vocals), Rick Kemp (bass, vocals), Richie Close (keyboards), Mick Dyche (guitar, vocals), Gary Wilson (drums, vocals)
Long Holiday/Information Station/Face To Face/Roll On the Day/ Back Into Cabaret/Commit The Crime/Friends/Reduced Circumstances/ Nothing But The Best/Love's Not Just A Word/Girls On the Town/ Anthem To Failure

Going For Glory (with The Answers, Kempire, UK, 1982)
Produced by Nick Griffiths (except "Deep In The Darkest Night", produced by David A. Stewart)
Musicians: Maddy Prior (vocals), Mick Dyche (guitars, backing vocals), Gary Wilson (drums, percussion, backing vocals), Richie Close (keyboards), Rick Kemp (bass and acoustic guitar, vocals, backing vocals), Annie Lennox (backing vocals, flute), Steve King (accordion), Howard Evans (trumpet, flugelhorn), Roger Williams (trombone, valve trombone, tuba)
After the Death/Saboteur/Morning Girls/Half Listening/Deep In The Darkest Night/Oh, No/God Squad/Trivial Hymn/Each Heart/ Hope Lies Now/Pater Noster/Allelujah

Year (Park Records, UK, 1993)
Produced by Maddy Prior
Musicians: Maddy Prior (vocals), Nick Holland (piano keyboards, Hammond BVs), Richard Lee (double bass), Rick Kemp (bass), Mick Dyche (acoustic guitars), Martin Loveday (cello), Liam Genockey (percussion), Andy Watts (shawms, recorder), John Dochary (bass, backing vocals)
Snowdrops-Birth/Swimming Song/Marigold-Harvest Home/ Red & Green/Long Shadows/Somewhere Along the Road/What Had You for Supper? /Saucy Sailor/The Fabled Hare/Deep In the Darkest Night/Boys Of Bedlam/Twa Corbies

Memento: The Best Of Maddy Prior (Park Records, UK, 1995)
This compilation, put together by John Dagnell at Park Records, draws on material from *Silly Sisters*, *Woman In The Wings*, *Changing*

Winds, *Hooked On Winning*, *Going For Glory*, *Year* and Maddy Prior &
Rick Kemp's *Happy Families*
After the Death/Long Shadows/The Grey Funnel Line/Baggy Pants/
Rose/Commit The Crime/Bewcastle/Mater Dolorosa/Woman In The
Wings/Face To Face/Doffin' Mistress/Mother And Child/Accappella
Stella/The Sovereign Prince/Deep In The Darkest Night/Alex/
Pater Noster/Allelujah

Flesh & Blood (Park Records, UK, 1997)
Produced by Nick Holland and Troy Donockley
Musicians: Maddy Prior (vocals), Nick Holland (keyboards, backing
vocals), Troy Donockley (uilleann pipes, electric and acoustic guitars,
whistles, cittern, backing vocals), Terl Bryant (drums and percussion),
Andy Crowdy (acoustic bass)
Sheath & Knife/The Rolling English Road/Honest Work/Finlandia/
Hind Horn/Bitter Withy/Who Am I/Cruel Mother/Boy On A Horse/
Jade/Brother Lawrence/The Laugh And The Kiss/The Point/
Heart Of Stone

Ravenchild (Park Records, UK, 1999)
Produced by Troy Donockley and Nick Holland
Musicians: Maddy Prior (vocals), Nick Holland (keyboards, backing
vocals), Troy Donockley (uilleann pipes, electric and acoustic guitars,
low whistle, tin whistle), Terl Bryant (drums and percussion), Nick Beggs
(Chapman stick)
Twankydillo/Bold Poachers/Boney/Scorched Earth/Loot/Rigs Of
The Time/In The Company Of Ravens/Young Bloods/The Masts Of
Morrigan/Rich Pickings/Ravenchild/Dance On the Wind/Great Silkie
Of Sule Skerry

A Rare Collection 1972-1996 (Raven Records, Australia, 1999)
This compilation features twenty rare Australian-only releases and live
performances, along with other previously unreleased material from the
Steeleye Span and Maddy Prior archives.
The King/Thomas The Rhymer/Elf Call/Gaudete/Lanercost/I Live Now
Where I Love/The Boar's Head Carol/Montrose/The Holly And The
Ivy/Like The Wind/I Have A Wish/Rag Doll/Rave On/Fire On The

Line/Somewhere Along The Road/Autumn To Spring Medley/Betsy
Bell And Mary Gray/Stookie/The Royal Forester/All Around My Hat

Ballads & Candles (Park Records, UK, 2000)
Recorded live in Cambridge, London and Warwick
Engineered by Richard Coulson (mobile) and Gareth Fox (live sound)
Musicians: Maddy Prior (vocals), June Tabor (vocals), Rose Kemp
(vocals), Steve Banks (drums, percussion and vocals), Troy Donockley
(electric guitar, uilleann pipes, low and tin whistle, cittern, vocals),
Nick Holland (keyboards, vocals), Rick Kemp (bass, vocals),
Peter Knight (violin)
The Blacksmith/Blood & Gold/The Boar's Head Carol/A Virgin Most
Pure/All In the Morning/Sing All Earth/Doffin' Mistress/Betsy Bell/
Hindhorn/Singing The Travels/Long Shadows/The King/Rose/
Mother And Child/Alex/My Husband's Got No Courage In Him/
Blackleg Miner/Padstow

Arthur The King (Park Records, UK, 2001)
Produced by Nick Holland and Troy Donockley
Musicians: Troy Donockley (electric guitar, uilleann pipes, low and tin
whistle, cittern), Nick Holland (keyboards)

Lionhearts (Park Records, UK, 2003)
Produced by Nick Holland and Troy Donockley
Musicians: Maddy Prior (vocals), Troy Donockley (uilleann pipes, electric
and acoustic guitars, bouzouki, backing vocals), Nick Holland (grand
piano, Fender Rhodes, Hammond X5 organ, Moog Prodigy, Paadwork,
backing vocals), Terl Bryant (drums and percussion), Katie Holland
(backing vocals)
Maman/John/Salah Ed-Din/Old Lion/Thomas/War Games/Salisbury
Plains/John Barleycorn/Yellow Handkerchief/Ship In Distress/Jupiter

Collections: A Very Best Of 1995 To 2005
(Park Records, UK, 2005)
This compilation is culled from *Flesh & Blood*, *Ravenchild*, *Arthur The
King* and *Lionhearts*, along with three tracks from Maddy Prior & The
Girls' *Bib & Tuck*, and live recordings from Tintagel and Liverpool on

the *Arthur The King* and *Lionhearts* tours respectively.
Sheath & Knife/Hind Horn/Twankydillo/Rigs Of The Time/In The
Company Of Ravens/Young Bloods/Brother Lawrence/Great Silkie Of
Sule Skerry/Once And Future King/Reynardine/Duke Of Marlborough/
Lark In The Morning/Maman/John/Salisbury Plains/Yellow
Handkerchief/John Barleycorn/Haul Her Away/Cropper Lads/
Liverpool Judies/Saucy Sailor/Deep In The Darkest Night/
The Fabled Hare

The Quest (Park Records, UK, 2007)
Recorded live at the Theatre Royal, Winchester
Musicians: Maddy Prior (vocals), Troy Donockley (uilleann pipes, electric
and acoustic guitar, bouzouki, low and tin whistle, backing vocals),
Nick Holland (keyboards), Terl Bryant (drums, percussion)
Sheath & Knife/Bitter Withy/The Quest/Joseph Was A Tin Man/
Maman/John/Fields Of The Cloth Of Gold/The Name Of Arthur/
Venturae Remembering/Hallows i/Queen And Sovereignty/Hallows ii/
Tribal Warriors/Hallows iii/Sentry/Hallows iv/Once And Future King/
Jupiter/Hind Horn/Ravenchild/Dance On The Wind/The Templar Knight

Seven For Old England (Park Records, UK, 2008)
Engineered by Tony Poole
Musicians: Maddy Prior (vocals), Benji Kirkpatrick (guitar, bouzouki,
banjo, vocals), Giles Lewin (ud, violin, viola, flute, harmonium, recorder,
vocals), John Kirkpatrick (button accordion, Anglo concertia, bass Anglo
concertina), John Banks (harp), Barney Morse-Brown (cello), Tony Poole
(12-string guitar)
Dives And Lazarus/Trooper's Nag/Jock Of Hazeldean/The Collier
Lad/Martinmas Time/Love Will Find Out The Way/In Sad And Ashy
Weeds/Bold General Wolfe/The Cuckoo/I Heard The Banns/Came Ye
From Newcastle/Trimdon Grange/Staines Morris/North Country Lass/
Come Again/Magpie

Hooked On Glory (Park Records, 2010)
This compilation features the albums, *Hooked On Winning* and *Going For
Glory*, in their entirety.

Singing Out

Maddy Prior & June Tabor

Silly Sisters (Chrysalis, UK, 1976)
Produced by Maddy Prior and Robin Black
Musicians: Maddy Prior (vocals), June Tabor (vocals), Martin Carthy
(guitar, drum), Nic Jones (fiddle, guitar), Tony Hall (melodeon),
Andy Irvine (mandolin, hurdy-gurdy), Johnny Moynihan (bouzouki,
whistle), Gabriel McKeon (uilleann pipes), Danny Thompson (bass),
John Gillaspie (bassoons, sopranino, bombard), Brian Golbey
(five-string fiddle)
Doffin' Mistress/Burning Of Auchindoon/Lass Of Loch Royal/
The Seven Joys Of Mary/My Husband's Got No Courage In Him/
Singing The Travels (Symondsbury Mummers)/Silver Whistle/The Grey
Funnel Line/Geordie/The Seven Wonders/Four Loom Weaver/
The Game Of Cards/Dame Durdan

No More To The Dance (Topic Records, UK, 1988)
Produced by Andrew Cronshaw
Musicians: Maddy Prior (vocals), June Tabor (vocals), Dan Ar Braz
(guitar), Huw Warren (keyboards), Jim Sutherland (percussion), Rick
Kemp (bass), Andrew Cronshaw (Chinese flutes, whistles, bombarde,
concertina), Patsy Seddon (Camac electro-harp, clarsachs),
Mary Macmaster (clarsachs), Bernard O'Neill (cello), Paul James
(soprano saxophone, half-long bagpipes), Nigel Eaton (hurdy-gurdy),
Mark Emerson (violin)
Blood And Gold-Mohacs/Cakes And Ale/Fine Horseman/How Shall I
Your True Love Know?/Hedger And Ditcher/Agincourt Carol-La Route
Au Beziers/The Barring Of The Door/What Will We Do?/Almost Every
Circumstances/The Old Miner

Maddy Prior & Rick Kemp

Happy Families (Park Records, UK, 1990)
Produced by Maddy Prior, Rick Kemp and Chris Baylis
Musicians: Maddy Prior (vocals), Rick Kemp (vocals, guitars, bass),
Simon Edwards (guitaron, Ashbory bass), Roy Dodds (drums,
percussion), Kim Burton (accordion, kaval, gajda), Nick Holland

(keyboard), Ian Kellet (keyboard), Chris Baylis (jet guitar), Pete Crowther (cello), Richard Lee (acoustic double bass)
Happy Families/Good Job/Rose/Mother And Child/Here Comes Midnight/Bewcastle/Who's Sorry Now? /Fire On The Line/Goodbye/ Alex/Low Flying/Happy Families (reprise)/Bewcastle (instrumental)

Maddy Prior & The Girls

Bib & Tuck (Park Records, UK, 2002)
Produced by Tony Poole with Maddy Prior, Rose Kemp and Abbie Lathe
Musicians: Maddy Prior (vocals), Rose Kemp (vocals), Abbie Lathe (vocals, guitar, keyboards, whistle)
Accappella Stella/I Am The World/A Stitch In Time/Hush Hush/Rain/ Sweet Thames Flow Softly/Down In The Valley/I Need You To Turn To/ Drop Of Blood/Sparkling Rills/True Colours/Blow Boys Blow/ The Dead Are Not Dead/Homeless/Haul Her Away/Cotton Fields/ Blow The Man Down/Cropper Lads/Doffin' Mistress/Liverpool Judies

Under The Covers (Park Records, UK, 2005)
Produced by Maddy Prior
Musicians: Maddy Prior (beatboxing), Abbie Lathe (beatboxing, piano), Claudia Gibson (vocals, beatboxing, keyboard, piano), Andy Watts (clarinet, recorders, bassoon, bass vocal), Giles Lewin (violins, shawms), Steve "Geezer" Watkins (electric guitar, beatboxing), Raph Mizraki (percussion, double bass), Barbabas Morse-Brown (cello), Tim Garside (percussion), Jane Griffiths (violin)
Ka-Ching/Under Your Thumb/One Way/Complex Person/Fear Of Life/Bend And Break/Sheela Na Gig/Great Divide/I Lost It/Get Out/ Postcards From Paraguay/A Perfect Indian/Love Is The Seventh Wave/ Slow Dance/Sword/Meeting Point/Melody Moon/Finnish Song/ Truth Of A Woman/Turning Point

Maddy Prior With Hannah James & Giles Lewin

3 For Joy (Park Records, UK, 2012)
Engineered by Bob Prowse
Musicians: Maddy Prior (vocals), Hannah James (vocals, accordion),

Giles Lewin (vocals, violin, viola, recorder, bagpipes)
Lock The Door Larriston-As A Thoiseach/The Raiders/Dacre's Gone
To War/Brisk Young Widow/Doffin' Mistress/Serving Girl's Holiday/
Of All The Birds/Nanine/Gankino Horo/Nauchila Sa Hubava Doina/
An Undoing World-Der Glater Bulgar/The Factory Girl-Buck Dance/
Wondrous Love/Oh, My Nanny

Maddy Prior & The Carnival Band

A Tapestry Of Carols (Saydisc, UK, 1987)
Produced by Gef Lucena and David Wilkins
Musicians: Maddy Prior (vocals), Bill Badley (lute, baroque guitar,
guitar, gittern, banjo, mandolin, mandocello, cittern, vocals), Andrew
Davis (double bass), Charles Fullbrook (small and medium tabors, Basel
trammel, glockenspiel, small bells, woodblocks, cowbell, triangle, antique
cymbals, tambourin provençal, vocals), Giles Lewin (violin, recorders,
vocals), Andrew Watts (Flemish bagpipes, bassoon, curtal, clarinet in C,
recorders, shawms, vocals)
Now The Holly Bears A Berry (The Sans Day Carol)/In Dulci Jubilo/
God Rest You, Merry Gentlemen/It Came Upon The Midnight Clear/
The Holly And The Ivy/Lully, Lullay, Thou Little Tiny Child (The
Coventry Carol)/Ding Dong Merrily On High/The Angel Gabriel
(Birjina gaztettobat zegoen)/Angels From The Realms Of Glory/Infant
Holy/A Virgin Most Pure/Unto Us A Boy Is Born/Rejoice And Be
Merry (The Gallery Carol)/Joseph Dearest/Personent Hodie/
On Christmas Night (The Sussex Carol)

Sing Lustily & With Good Courage (Saydisc, UK, 1990)
Produced by Gef Lucena and David Wilkins
Musicians: Maddy Prior (vocals), Bill Badley (lute, guitar (19th century
original), steel-string guitar, mandolin, mandocello, banjo, vocals),
Charles Fullbrook (tabors, side drum, bass drum, cymbals, wood blocks,
cow bell, vocals), Jub Davis (double bass), Giles Lewin (violin, recorder,
vocals), Andy Watts (curtal, bassoon (19th century original), clarinet in C,
recorder, vocals)
Who Would True Valour See/Rejoice Ye Shining Worlds/O Thou Who
Camest From Above/Lo He Comes With Clouds Descending/

Discographies

How Firm A Foundation/O For A Thousand Tongues To Sing/As Pants
The Hart/The God Of Abraham Praise/The Twenty-Ninth Of May Or
The Jovial Beggars, Monkland/Light Of The World/All Hail The Pow'r Of
Jesus' Name/Lord, In The Morning/Away With Our Sorrows And Care/
Christ The Lord Is Ris'n Today/O Worship The King/And Can It Be?

Carols And Capers (Park Records, UK, 1991)
Produced by Andrew Watts and Chris Baylis
Musicians: Maddy Prior (vocals), Andy Watts (shawms, curtal, clarinet,
recorders, Breughel bagpipes, vocals), Giles Lewin (shawm, fiddle,
recorders, medieval bagpipes, tin whistle, vocals), Bill Badley (acoustic
and electric guitar, lute, mandolin, banjo, vocals), Jub Davis (bass),
Raph Mizraki (drums, percussion, bells, cello, vocals)
The Boar's Head Carol, Away In A Manger, My Dancing Day, Monsieur
Charpentier's Christmas Stomp/See Amid The Winter's Snow/A Boy
Was Born/Poor Little Jesus/Turkey In The Straw-Whiskey Before
Breakfast/Wassail!/Joy To The World/Cradle Song/Shepherds Rejoice/
Old Joe Clark/Ane Sang Of The Birth Of Christ (Balulalow), Monsieur
Charpentier's Christmas Swing/Quem Pastores/While Shepherds
Watched/I Saw Three Ships

Hang Up Sorrow And Care (Park Records, UK, 1995)
Produced by Andrew Watts and Bill Badley
Musicians: Maddy Prior (vocals), Bill Badley (lute, baroque guitar,
acoustic and electric modern guitars, banjo, mandolin, vocals), Jub Davis
(double bass, vocals), Giles Lewin (violin, recorder, hoboy, mandolin,
vocals), Raf Mizraki (drums, percussion, cello, Hammond organ, vocals),
Andrew Watts (Flemish bagpipes, shalmes, curtails, recorders, melodic,
kazoo, vocals)
The Prodigal's Resolution/Playford Tunes/The World Is Turned Upside
Down/The Jovial Beggar/The Leathern Bottel/Iantha/An Thou Were My
Ain Thing/Oh! That I Had But A Fine Man/Now O Now I Needs Must
Part/Man Is For The Woman Made/A Northern Catch-Little Barley
Corne/Granny's Delight-My Lady Foster's Delight/A Round Of Three
Country Dances In One/Youths' The Season Made For Joys/In the Days
Of My Youth/Never Weatherbeaten Saile/Old Simon The King

Singing Out

Carols At Christmas (Park Records, UK, 1998)
This live album was recorded during the December 1997 tour by Maddy
Prior & The Carnival Band.
Engineered by Gareth Fox Williams and Richard Coulson (live) and
Steve Watkins (studio)
Musicians: Maddy Prior (vocals), Andy Watts (shawms, curtal, clarinet,
recorders, Breughel bagpipes, vocals), Giles Lewin (shawm, fiddle,
recorders, medieval bagpipes, tin whistle, vocals), Bill Badley (acoustic
and electric guitar, lute, mandolin, banjo, vocals), Jub Davis (bass, vocals),
Raf Mizraki (drums, taber, percussion, bells, cello, vocals), Rose Kemp
(vocals)

This Is The Truth-Shepherds, Arise! (Sing, Sing All Earth)/
Tomorrow Shall Be My Dancing Day/Lully, Lullay, Thou Little Tiny
Child (The Coventry Carol)/Monsieur Charpentier's Christmas Stomp/
Ding Dong Merrily On High/Let An Anthem Of Praise/Angels From
The Realms Of Glory/Watts' Cradle Song/Wassail!/The Boar's Head
Carol/Away In A Manger/In Dulci Jubilo/Now The Holy Bears A Berry
(The Sans Day Carol)/Monsieur Charpentier's Christmas Swing/
I Saw Three ships/Poor Little Jesus/Personent Hodie

Gold, Frankincense & Myrrh (Park Records, UK, 2001)
Produced by John Dagnell
Musicians: Maddy Prior (vocals), Bill Badley (renaissance and baroque
lutes, guitar, mandolin, vocals), Steve Banks (djembe, talking drum, saz,
violin, vocals), Jub Davis (modern and baroque double basses, percussion,
vocals), Giles Lewin (violin, viola, recorders, flute, shawm, vocals), Raph
Mizraki (ud, saz, darabuka, balafon, percussion, vocals), Andy Watts
(shawm, recorders, clarinet, Turkish clarinet, bassoon, vocals)

Melchior/Caspar/Balthazar/Journey To Jericho/Melima/Journey To
Bethlehem And Song Of the Animals/Welcome Stranger/Song Of
Angels/The Oxen/The Carnal And The Crane/Rorate Coeli De Super/
Entre Le Boeuf Et L'Ane Gris/Hark! Hark! What News/
Bethlehem Down

Discographies

An Evening of Carols And Capers (Park Records, UK, 2005)
This live album was recorded at Oxford Town Hall during the 2003
Christmas tour by Maddy Prior & The Carnival Band.
Executively produced by John Dagnell
Musicians: Maddy Prior (vocals), Andy Watts (shawms, curtal, clarinets,
recorders, Breughel bagpipes, vocals), Giles Lewin (shawm, fiddle,
recorders, medieval bagpipes, tin whistle, vocals), Jub Davis (bass),
Steve Banks (drums, percussion, bells, fiddle, vocals), Raph Mizraki
(acoustic and electric guitars, vocals)
Masters In This Hall/The Sans Day Carol/God Rest You, Merry
Gentlemen/This Endris Night/Monsieur Charpentier's Christmas
Stomp/Let An Anthem Of Praise/The Oxen/Balthazar/Round Of
The Animals/Melima/It Came Upon The Midnight Clear/The Sussex
Carol/Watts' Cradle Song/Vals Musette/Entre Le Boeuf/Monsieur
Charpentier's Christmas Swing/Dratenik (Tinker Polka)/The Carnal
And The Crane/Ding Dong Merrily On High/Angels From The Realms
of Glory/Hark, Hark/While Shepherds Watched

**Paradise Found: A Celebration Of Charles Wesley
1707–1788** (Park Records, UK, 2007)
Engineered by Steve Watkins
Musicians: Maddy Prior (vocals), Andy Watts (clarinet, bassoon, recorder,
vocals), Giles Lewin (violin, recorder, vocals), Steve Banks (drum, violin,
vocals), Jub Davis (double bass, vocals), Steno Vitale (guitar, mandolin),
Bill Badley (lute
Arm Of The Lord, Awake!/Hail The Day That Sees Him Rise/O For A
Heart To Praise My God/I Know That My Redeemer Lives/Come Away
To The Skies/Jesu, If Still The Same Thou Art/Let Heaven And Earth
Agree/My God I Am Thine/Lord Divine, All Loves Excelling/
Ye Servants Of God/Dead! Dead! The Child I Lov'd So Well/Soldiers Of
Christ Arise/Jesu, Lover Of My Soul/Come O Thou Traveller Unknown/
Come On My Partners In Distress

Ringing The Changes (Park Records, UK, 2007)
Engineered by Steve Watkins
Musicians: Maddy Prior (vocals), Andy Watts (shawm, C clarinet,
Turkish G clarinet, recorder, melodic, vocals), Giles Lewin (violin,

recorder, shawm, vocals), Steve Banks (drums, Latin percussion, djembe, violin, guitar, vocals), Jub Davis (double bass, vocals), Steno Vitale (guitar, mandolin, vocals), Terry Jones (vocals)
Wake Up!/Blue Pearl/Bright Evening Star/Carol (There Was A Boy)/ Lachrimae Amoris/The Gift/Stuff/Bring Us In Good Ale/Ring The Bell, Watchman!/The Changing Face Of Christmas/The Quiet Way Home/ Home/The Undefeated Sun/A Latin Latin Christmas

Vaughan Williams Carols, Songs & Hymns (Park Records, UK, 2010)
Engineered by Mark Lee and Tony Poole
Musicians: Maddy Prior (vocals), Steve Banks (percussion, violin, vocals), Jub Davis (double bass, vocals), Giles Lewin (violin, viola, recorder, vocals), Steno Vitale (electric and acoustic guitar, mandolin), Andy Watts (clarinet, bassoon, recorder, shawm, vocals)
The Golden Carol/Blake's Cradle Song/The Blessed Son Of God/ Snow In The Street/Wither's Rocking Hymn/Drinking Song (Back And Side Go Bare)/Whither Must I Wander?/The Willow Whistle/Linden Lea/The Divine Image/The Woodcutter's Song/Come Down O Love Divine/Fierce Raged The Tempest/At The Name Of Jesus/ Into The Woods My Master Went/The Night Is Come/God Be With You Till We Meet Again

A Christmas Caper: The Best Of Maddy Prior & The Carnival Band (Park Records, UK, 2012)
This compilation features 22 songs from over a quarter century of Maddy Prior & The Carnival Band.
Mastered by Bob Prowse
Additional Musicians: Louisa Fuller (violin), Benjamin Kaminski (viola), Kath Sharman (cello), John Spiers (melodeon), Peter Cowdrey (trombone)
I Saw Three Ships/While Shepherds Watched/Angels From The Realms Of Glory/God Rest You, Merry Gentlemen/Monsieur Charpentier's Christmas Swing/Joy To The World/See Amid The Winter's Snow/ Poor Little Jesus/Blake's Cradle Song/Coventry Carol/The Boar's Head/ Ding Dong Merrily On High/The Holly And The Ivy/Personent Hodie/ Cradle Song/Bright Evening Star/Hark! Hark! What News/

Away In A Manger/The Carnal And The Crane/Bring Us In Good Ale/
La Danse Carree/The Quiet Way Home

June Tabor

Airs And Graces (Topic Records, UK, 1976)
Produced by Paul Brown
Musicians: June Tabor (vocals), Nic Jones (acoustic guitar, fiddle),
Tony Hall (melodeon), Jon Gillaspie (piano, organ, roxichord, bassoon,
sopranino)
While Gamekeepers Lie Sleeping/Plains Of Waterloo/Bonny May/
Reynardine/And The Band Played Waltzing Matilda/Young Waters/
Waly Waly/The Merchant's Son/Queen Among The Heather/
Pull Down Lads

Ashes And Diamonds (Topic Records, UK, 1977)
Produced by Paul Brown
Musicians: June Tabor (vocals), Jon Gillaspie (synthesiser, piano,
recorder), Nic Jones (fiddle, guitar), Tony Hall (melodeon), Doug Morter
(electric guitar), Rick Kemp (bass), Nigel Pegrum (drums)
Reynard the Fox/The Devil And Bailiff McGlynn/Street Of Forbes/Lord
Maxwell's Last Goodnight/Now I'm Easy/Clerk Saunders/
The Earl Of Aboyne/Lisbon/The Easter Tree/Cold And Raw/
No Man's Land-Flowers Of The Forest

Abyssinians (Topic Records, UK, 1983)
Produced by Andrew Cronshaw
Musicians: June Tabor (vocals), Dave Bristow (keyboards),
Martin Simpson (guitar), Ric Sanders (violin)
The Month Of January/The Scarecrow/One Night As I Lay On My
Bed/She Moves Among Men (The Bar Maid's Song)/Lay This Body
Down/A Smiling Shore/The Bonny Boy/Never Never Thought My Love
Would Leave Me/The Bonny Hind/The Fiddle And The Drum

Aqaba (Topic Records, UK, 1988)
Produced by Andrew Cronshaw
Musicians: June Tabor (vocals), Huw Warren (piano), Martin Simpson

(guitar, baritone guitar, mandola), Ric Sanders (electric violin),
Dave Bristow (Yamaha DX7 and WX7 synthesisers), Ian Blake (bass
clarinet)
The Old Man's Song (Don Quixote)/Searching For Lambs/The Bank
Of Red Roses/Where Are You Tonight, I Wonder?/Aqaba/Verdi Cries/
The Grazier's Daughter/Seven Summers/Mayn Rue Plats (My Resting
Place)/The King Of Rome

Some Other Time (Hannibal Records, UK, 1989)
Produced by Joe Boyd
Musicians: June Tabor (vocals), Huw Warren (piano, cello),
Mark Lockheart (saxophones), Danny Thompson (bass),
Bosco de Olivera (percussion)
 Some Other Time/Night And Day/You Don't Know What Love Is/
Body And Soul/This Is Always/I've Got You Under My Skin/
The Man I Love/Meditation/Sophisticated Lady/Round Midnight

Aspects (Conifer Records, UK, 1990)
This is a compilation culled from June's solo albums, *Airs And Graces*,
Ashes And Diamonds, *Abyssinians* and *Aqaba*, *A Cut Above* (with Martin
Simpson), *No More To The Dance* (with Maddy Prior), and *Freedom And
Rain* (with The Oysterband).
Strange Affair/Almost Every Circumstance/Bonny May/The
Scarecrow/A Smiling Shore/Flash Company/What Will We Do?/
While Gamekeepers Lie Sleeping/Aqaba/Now I'm Easy/
Cakes And Ale/Pull Down Lads/Mrs Rita/Pain Or Paradise

Angel Tiger (Cooking Vinyl, UK, 1992)
Produced by John Ravenhall
Musicians: June Tabor (vocals), Huw Warren (piano, cello, accordion),
Mark Emerson (violin, viola, accordion, piano), Mark Lockheart (clarinet,
tenor and soprano saxophone), Dudley Phillips (double bass), Bosco de
Oliveira (percussion)
Hard Love/Joseph Cross/Sudden Waves/Rumours Of War/
All Our Trades Are Gone/Happed In Mist/The Doctor Calls/
Let No Man Steal Your Thyme/All This Useless Beauty/Ten Thousand
Miles/Blind Step Away/Elephant

Discographies

Anthology (Music Club, UK, 1993)

This compilation features tracks from June's solo albums, *Airs And Graces*, *Ashes And Diamonds*, *Abyssinians*, *Aqaba* and *Angel Tiger*, as well as from *A Cut Above* (with Martin Simpson) and *Freedom And Rain* (with The Oysterband).

Mississippi Summer/Verdi Cries/Strange Affair/She Moves Among Men (The Bar Maid's Song)/Lay This Body Down/And the Band Played Waltzing Matilda/Night Comes In/The King Of Rome/Lisbon/ The Month Of January/Hard Love/Dark-Eyed Sailor/Heather Down The Moor/Cold And Raw/Sudden Waves/No Man's Land-Flowers Of The Forest

Against The Streams (Cooking Vinyl, UK, 1994)

Produced by John Ravenhall

Musicians: June Tabor (vocals), Huw Warren (piano, cello), Mark Emerson (viola, violin, piano accordion), Andy Cutting (diatonic accordion), Mark Lockheart (clarinet, tenor and soprano saxophone), Dudley Phillips (double bass)

Shameless Love/I Want To Vanish/False, False/Pavanne/He Fades Away/The Irish Girl/Apples And Potatoes/Beauty And The Beast: An Anniversary/The Turn Of The Road/Windy City/Waiting For The Lark

Aleyn (Topic Records, UK, 1997)

Produced by John Ravenhall

Musicians: June Tabor (vocals), Andy Cutting (diatonic accordion), Mark Emerson (violin, viola), Mark Lockheart (clarinet, tenor and soprano saxophones), Dudley Phillips (double bass), Huw Warren (piano, piano accordion)

The Great Valerio/I Wonder What's Keeping My True Love Tonight?/ No Good At Love/Bentley & Craig/The Fiddler/April Morning/ Di Nakht/The Fair Maid Of Islington/Go From My Window/ A Proper Sort Of Gardener/Johnny O'Bredislee/Shallow Brown

On Air (Strange Fruit, UK, 1998)

This is a compilation of recordings from June's BBC sessions.

White Rabbit/The Furze Field/Young Allan/As I Roved Out/ The Banks Of The Sweet Dundee/Terror Time/This Wheel's On Fire/

Lord Bateman/The Overgate/Derry Gaol/Short Jacket And White
Trousers/All Along The Watchtower

A Quiet Eye (Topic Records, UK, 1999)
Produced by John Ravenhall
Musicians: June Tabor (vocals), Huw Warren (piano), Mark Bassey
(trombone), Liam Kirkman (trombone), Richard Iles (trumpet),
Jim Rattigan (French horn), Richard Bolton (cello), Richard Fox (tuba),
Dudley Phillips (double bass), Andy Schofield (clarinet, alto saxophone),
Iain Dixon (bass clarinet, clarinet), Mark Emerson (violin, viola),
Roy Dodds (percussion), Mark Lockheart (clarinet, tenor and soprano
saxophones)
The Gardener/A Place Called England/I Will Put My Ship In Order/
I'll Be Seeing You/Out Of Winter-Waltzing's For Dreamers/Pharaoh/
Must I Be Bound?/The Writing Of Tipperary-It's A Long Way To
Tipperary/The First Time Ever I Saw Your Face/The Water Is Wide-St
Agnes-Jeannie And Jamie

Rosa Mundi (Topic Records, UK, 2001)
Produced by John Ravenhall
Musicians: June Tabor (vocals), Huw Warren (piano), Mark Emerson
(violin, viola), Richard Bolton (cello)
Roses Of Picardy/Belle Rose/Deep In Love/O My Luve's Like A Red
Red Rose/Rose In June/Paint Me, Redoute/Rhosyn Wyn-Winterrose/
The Rose Is White, The Rose Is Red-Dargason/The Crown Of Roses
(Tchaikowsky's Legend)/Barbry Ellen/Maybe Then I'll Be A Rose

Echo Of Hooves (Topic Records, UK, 2003)
Engineered by Charlie Beresford
Musicians: June Tabor (vocals), Huw Warren (piano, cello, piano
accordion), Mark Emerson (violin, viola, piano), Tim Harries (double
bass), Martin Simpson (guitar), Kathryn Tickell (Northumbrian pipes)
Bonnie James Campbell/The Duke Of Athole's Nurse/
The Battle Of Otterburn/Lord Maxwell's Last Goodnight/
Hughie Graeme/The Border Widow's Lament/Fair Margaret And Sweet
William/Rare Willie/Young Johnstone/The Cruel Mother/
Sir Patrick Spens

Discographies

The Definitive Collection (Highpoint, UK, 2003)
This compilation draws on material from June's solo albums, *Airs And Graces*, *Ashes And Diamonds*, *Abyssinians*, *Aqaba*, *Aleyn*, *A Quiet Eye* and *Rosa Mundi*, *A Cut Above* (with Martin Simpson), *No More To The Dance* (with Maddy Prior), *The Transports* (*A Ballad Opera* with Peter Bellamy) and Ashley Hutchings' *Street Cries*.
Where Are You Tonight, I Wonder?/Queen Among The Heather/ Streets Of Forbes/Unicorns/I Never Thought My Love Would Leave Me/The Barring Of The Door/The Leaves In The Woodland/ Maybe Then I'll Be A Rose/The Water Is Wide/Lord Maxwell's Last Goodnight/The Scarecrow/Go From My Window/While Gamekeepers Lie Sleeping/These Cold Lips/Shallow Brown

Always (Topic Records, UK, 2005)
This comprehensive anthology of June's career includes many rare, live and previously unreleased recordings.
The Seeds Of Love/The King Of Rome/Hard Love/Casey's Last Ride/ What Will We Do?/Skewball/While Gamekeepers Lie Sleeping/ The Week Before Easter/Strange Affair/Sir Patrick Spens/ Gypsum Davey/Buried In Kilkenny/Behind The Wall/Zaida's Poem/ Young Johnstone/Mississippi Summer/A Place Called England/ I Never Thought You Would Leave Me/Beat The Retreat/ Fine Horseman/The Overgate/The Fair Maid Of Wallington/ Meditation/Geordie/All This Useless Beauty/Love Henry-The Cherokee Shuffle/Illusions/Four Loom Weaver/I Will Put My Ship In Order/ Cold And Raw-Down The Hill/The Nurse, Dorothy Nicol-The Long Long Trail-The Reaper/And The Band Played Waltzing Matilda/ Maybe Then I'll Be A Rose/April Morning/Johnny O'Bredislee/Singing The Travels/Waiting For The Lark/Ten Thousand Miles/Hunting The Cutty Wren/Willie Taylor/Bonny May/Aqaba/Anachie Gordon/ Reynardine/Dashing Away With The Smoothing Iron/Pharaoh/Belle Rose/Will Ye Go To Flanders?/Shallow Brown/Now I'm Easy/Mrs Rita/ All Tomorrow's Parties/The Wind And Rain/Bonnie James Campbell/ A Proper Sort Of Gardener/The Royal Oak/False, False/Roseville Fair/ Eights And Aces/The Baker/This Is Always/Queen Cruelty/Joe Peel/All Our Trades Are Gone/Virginia's Bloody Soil/Hug Pine/ The Late Passenger-Unicorns

At The Wood's Heart (Topic Records, UK, 2005)
Produced by Andrew Cronshaw
Musicians: June Tabor (vocals), Huw Warren (piano), Martin Simpson
(guitar), Andy Cutting (diatonic accordion), Mark Emerson (viola and
violin), Mark Lockheart (tenor and soprano saxophones), Tim Harries
(double bass), Iain Ballamy (tenor saxophone)
The Banks Of The Sweet Primroses/The Broomfield Wager/
Ah! The Sighs/Now Welcome Summer/Heart Like A Wheel/
Johnny Johnny/Oh! Alas, I Am In Love/Do Nothing 'Till You Hear
From Me/Les Choses Les Plus Simples/She's Like The Swallow/
The Cloud Factory/Lie Near Me

Apples (Topic Records, UK, 2007)
Engineered by Martin Levan
Musicians: June Tabor (vocals), Andy Cutting (diatonic accordion),
Mark Emerson (piano, violin, viola), Tim Harries (double bass)
The Dancing/Miss Lindsay Barker/The Old Garden Gate/
The Auld Beggarman/The Rigs Of Rye/I Love My Love/Soldiers Three/
Speak Easy/Au Logis De Mon Pere/Standing In Line/Ce Fu En Mai/
My Love Came To Dublin/Send Us A Quiet Night

Ashore (Topic Records, UK, 2011)
Musicians: June Tabor (vocals), Andy Cutting (diatonic accordion), Mark
Emerson (violin, viola), Tim Harries (double bass), Huw Warren (piano)
Finisterre/The Bleacher Lassie Of Kelvinhaugh/The Grey Funnel Line/
Le Vingt-Cinquiemme Du Mois d'Octobre/Shipbuilding/Jamaica/The
Great Selkie Of Sule Skerry/Winter Comes In-Vidlin Voe/
The Oggie Man/I'll Go And Enlist For A Sailor/The Brean Lament/
Le Petit Navire/Across The Wide Ocean

June Tabor with Martin Simpson

A Cut Above (Topic Records, UK, 1980)
Produced by Paul Brown
Musicians: June Tabor (vocals), Martin Simpson (guitars), Ric Sanders
(violin), Dave Bristow (piano, synthesiser), Jon Davies (bass), The
Prunettes, featuring Louisa Livingstone, Dik Cadbury, Martin Simpson,

Discographies

Ric Sanders, Dave Bristow, Paul Brown (vocals)
Admiral Benbow/Davy Lowston/Flash Company/Number Two Top
Seam/Strange Affair/Heather Down The Moor/Joe Peel/Le Roi Renaud/
Riding Down To Portsmouth/Unicorns

June Tabor & The Oysterband

Freedom And Rain (Cooking Vinyl, UK, 1990)
Produced by The Oysterband
June Tabor (vocals), Alan Prosser (guitar, mandolin, psaltery, vocals),
Russell Lax (drums, percussion), Chopper (bass, cello), Ian Telfer (fiddle,
viola, concertina, organ), John Jones (melodeon, accordion, vocals),
Gavin Sharp (tenor saxophone), John Hart (bass trombone), Neil Yates
(trumpet)
Mississippi Summer/Lullaby Of London/Night Comes In/
Valentine's Day Is Over/All Tomorrow's Parties/Dives And Lazarus/
Dark-Eyed Sailor/Pain Or Paradise/Susie Clelland/Finisterre

Ragged Kingdom (Topic Records, UK, 2011)
Produced by Al Scott
Musicians: June Tabor (vocals), John Jones (vocals, melodeon), Ray
Cooper (cello, mandolin, bass guitar, harmonium, vocals), Dil Davies
(drums), Alan Prosser (guitars, kantele, fiddle, vocals), Ian Telfer (fiddle),
Al Scott (bass guitar, mandola)
The Bonny Bunch Of Roses/That Was My Veil/My Son David/
Love Will Tear Us Apart/(When I Was No But) Sweet Sixteen/Judas (Was
A Red-Headed Man)/If My Love Loves Me/The Hills Of Shiloh/Fountains
Flowing/The Leaves Of Life/Seven Curses/The Dark End Of The Street

Quercus

Quercus (ECM Records, UK, 2013)
Produced by Manfred Eicher, Iain Ballamy and Huw Warren
Musicians: June Tabor (vocals), Iain Ballamy (tenor and soprano
saxophones), Huw Warren (piano)
Lassie Lie Near Me/Come Away Death/As I Roved Out/The Lads In
Their Hundreds/Teares/Near But Far Away/Brigg Fair/Who Wants The

Evening Rose/This Is Always/A Tale From History (The Shooting)/
All I Ask Of You

Richard & Linda Thompson

I Want To See The Bright Lights Tonight (Island Records,
UK, 1974)
Produced by Richard Thompson and John Wood
Musicians: Richard Thompson (vocals, guitar, hammered dulcimer,
mandolin, whistle, piano, electric piano, harmonium), Linda Thompson
(vocals), Timmy Donald (drums), Pat Donaldson (bass), John Kirkpatrick
(Anglo concertina and accordion), Simon Nicol (dulcimer), Brian Gulland
(krummhorn), Richard Harvey (krummhorn), Royston Wood (backing
vocals), Trevor Lucas (backing vocals), The CWS Silver Band (brass)
When I Get To The Border/The Calvary Cross/Withered And Died/
I Want To See The Bright Lights Tonight/Down Where The Drunkards
Roll/We Sing Hallalujah/Has He Got A Friend For Me?/
The Little Beggar Girl/The End Of The Rainbow/The Great Valerio

Hokey Pokey (Island Records, UK, 1974)
Produced by Richard Thompson and Simon Nicol
Musicians: Richard Thompson (guitar, vocals, mandolin, hammered
dulcimer, electric dulcimer, piano), Linda Thompson (vocals), Timi
Donald (drums), Pat Donaldson (bass guitar), Simon Nicol (guitar, piano,
Hammond organ, vocals), John Kirkpatrick (accordion), Ian Whiteman
(piano, Calliope), Sidonie Goossens (harp), Aly Bain (fiddle), The CWS
Silver Band (brass)
Hokey Pokey/I'll Regret It All in the Morning/Smiffy's Glass Eye/
The Egypt Room/Never Again/Georgie On A Spree/Old Man Inside
A Young Man/The Sun Never Shines On The Poor/A Heart Needs A
Home/Mole In A Hole

Pour Down Like Silver (Island Records, UK, 1975)
Produced by Richard Thompson and John Wood
Musicians: Richard Thompson (vocals, guitar), Linda Thompson (vocals),
Pat Donaldson (bass), Dave Pegg (bass), Timmy Donald (drums),
Dave Mattacks (drums), John Kirkpatrick (button accordion, Anglo
concertina), Nic Jones (fiddle), Aly Bain (fiddle), Henry Lowther

Discographies

(trumpet), Ian Whiteman (concert flute, shakuhachi)
Streets Of Paradise/For Shame Of Doing Wrong/The Poor Boy Is Taken
Away/Night Comes In/Jet Plane In A Rocking Chair/Beat The Retreat/
Hard Luck Stories/Dimming Of The Day-Dargai

First Light (Chrysalis Records, UK, 1978)
Produced by John Wood and Richard Thompson
Musicians: Linda Thompson (vocals), Richard Thompson (vocals, guitar,
mandolin, hammered dulcimer, Roland guitar, synthesiser, whistle), Andy
Newark (drums), Willie Weeks (bass), Neil Larsen (keyboards), Simon
Nicol (guitar, dulcimer), Chris Karen (drums), Dave Mattacks (drums),
Dolores Keane (whistle), John Kirkpatrick (button accordion), Dave
Brady, Heather Brady, Dave Burland, Bill Caddick, Philippa Clare, Julie
Covington, Andy Fairweather Low, Trevor Lucas, Ian Matthews, Maddy
Prior, Peta Walsh (all backing vocals)
Restless Highway/Sweet Surrender/Don't Let A Thief Steal Into Your
Heart/The Choice Wife/Died For Love/Strange Affair/Layla/Pavanne/
House Of Cards/First Light

Sunnyvista (Chrysalis Records, UK, 1979)
Produced by John Wood and Richard Thompson
Musicians: Richard Thompson (vocals, guitar, mandolin, hammered
dulcimer, Roland guitar synthesiser), Linda Thompson (vocals),
Michael Spencer-Arscott (drums), Tim Donald (drums and percussion),
Dave Pegg (bass), Pat Donaldson (bass), Simon Nicol (acoustic and
electric guitars), John Kirkpatrick (accordion, triangle), Sue Harris (oboe,
hammered dulcimer), Pete Wingfield (keyboards), Rabbit Bundrick
(keyboards), Louis Jardine (percussion), Dave Mattacks (drums),
Bruce Lynch (bass), Kate and Anna McGarrigle (backing vocals),
Glenn Tilbrook (backing vocals), Julian Littman (backing vocals), Marc
Ellington (backing vocals), Gerry Rafferty (backing vocals),
Olive Simpson (backing vocals), Nicole Tibbels (backing vocals),
Lindsay Benton (backing vocals), Hafsa Abdul Jabbas (backing vocals),
Abdu Rahim (backing vocals)
Civilisation/Borrowed Time/Saturday Rolling Around/You're Going To
Need Somebody/Why Do You Turn Your Back?/Sunnyvista/
Lonely Hearts/Sisters/Justice In The Streets/Traces Of My Love

Shoot Out The Lights (Hannibal, USA, 1982)
Produced by Joe Boyd
Musicians: Richard Thompson (vocals, lead guitar, accordion, hammered
dulcimer), Linda Thompson (vocals), Simon Nicol (rhythm guitar),
Dave Pegg (bass), Pete Zorn (bass, backing vocals), Dave Mattacks
(drums), The Watersons (backing vocals), Stephen Corbett (cornet),
Brian Jones (cornet), Phil Goodwin (tuba), Stephen Barnett (trombone),
Mark Cutts (trombone)
Don't Renege On Our Love/Walking On A Wire/Man In Need/
Just The Motion/Shoot Out The Lights/Back Street Slide/Did She Jump
Or Was She Pushed?/Wall Of Death

**The End Of The Rainbow: An Introduction To Richard
& Linda Thompson** (Island Records, UK, 2000)
This compilation features songs from Richard's *Henry The Human Fly!*
alongside songs from Richard and Linda's *I Want To See The Bright Lights
Tonight, Hokey Pokey* and *Pour Down Like Silver.*
Roll Over Vaughan Williams/The Poor Ditching Boy/When I Get
To The Border/Withered And Died/I Want To See The Bright Lights
Tonight/Down Where The Drunkards Roll/The End Of The Rainbow/
The Great Valerio/Hokey Pokey (The Ice Cream Song)/Never Again/
A Heart Needs A Home/For Shame Of Doing Wrong/Night Comes In/
Beat The Retreat/Dimming Of the Day-Dargai/Calvary Cross

Linda Thompson

One Clear Moment (Warner Bros Records, USA, 1985)
Produced by Hugh Murphy
Musicians: Linda Thompson (vocals), Betsy Cook (musical director,
backing vocals, keyboards), Jerry Donahue, Albert Lee, Liam Genockey,
Gary Twigg, Stephen Lipson, Fran Breen, Chris Baylis, Kevin Powell
Can't Stop The Girl/One Clear Moment/Telling Me Lies/In Love With
The Flame/Les Trois Beaux Oiseaux De Paradis/Take Me On The Subway/
Best Of Friends/Hell, High Water And Heartache/Just Enough To Keep
Me Hanging On/Lover Won't You Throw Me A Line/Only A Boy

Dreams Fly Away: A History Of Linda Thompson

(Hannibal Records, UK, 1996)

This compilation features material from Richard & Linda Thompson,
The Home Service and Linda solo.

Produced by Hugh Murphy, John Wood and Richard Thompson
Lonely Hearts/Walking On A Wire/I Live Not Where I Love/
Sometimes It Happens/For Shame Of Doing Wrong/Talking Like
A Man/Sisters/Shay Fan Yan Ley/One Clear Moment/First Light/
Pavanne/Many Dreams Must Fly Away/I Want To See The Bright
Lights Tonight/The Great Valerio/Insult To Injury/The Poor Boy Is
Taken Away/Blackwaterside/Telling Me Lies/I'm A Dreamer/
Dimming Of The Day

Give Me A Sad Song (Fledg'ling Records, UK, 2001)

This compilation pulls together unreleased demos and rare tracks
recorded between 1970 and 1986, with musicians including Richard
Thompson, Martin Carthy, Andy Roberts, Neil Innes, Gerry Conway,
John Taylor, Dave Richards and Betsy Cook.

Story Of Isaac/Down River/Fire And Rain/From A City Balcony/
Get Back/Sometimes It Happens/Embroidered Butterflies/After Frost/
You Missed The Sunflowers At Their Height/Restless Boy/The World Is
A Wonderful Place/Abandoned/Hell, Highwater & Heartache/
Her Father Was A Sailor/When I Mention Love/Give Me A Sad Song/
Aimless Love

Fashionably Late (Topic Records, UK, 2002)

Produced by Edward Haber
Musicians: Linda Thompson (lead and harmony vocals, tambourine,
guitar), Teddy Thompson (acoustic guitar, lead and harmony vocals)
Kamila Thompson (harmony vocals, backing vocals), Richard Thompson
(electric guitar, backing vocals), Danny Thompson (double bass, acro
bass), Jeff Berman (snare drum, tambourine), John Doyle (acoustic
guitar), Richard Greene (fiddle), Van Dyke Parks (accordion, Hammond
B-3 organ), Kate Rusby (acoustic guitar, harmony vocals), Jerry Donahue
(electric guitar), Geraint Watkins (Hammond B-3 organ), Peter Adams
(keyboard), Mike Rivard (electric bass), Dave Mattacks (drums), Rufus
Wainwright (backing vocals), Martha Wainwright (backing vocals),

John McCusker (cittern), Andy Cutting (diatonic accordion),
Rori McFarlane (fretless electric bass), Kathryn Tickell (Northumbrian
small pipes), Eliza Carthy (fiddle, harmony vocal), Phil Pickett
(crumhorns), Dave Pegg (acoustic bass guitar, mandolin), Chris Cutler
(drums), Martin Carthy (acoustic guitar), Howard Gott (violin),
Ruth Gottlieb (violin), Sophia Sirota (viola), Robert Spriggs (viola),
Sarah Wilson (cello), Andy Waterworth (double bass), Robert Kirby
(string arrangement)
Dear Mary/Miss Murray/All I See/Nine Stone Rig/No Telling/
Evona Darling/The Banks Of The Clyde (For Brian)/Weary Life/Paint
& Powder Beauty/Dear Old Man Of Mine

Versatile Heart (Rounder Records, UK, 2007)
Produced by Edward Haber
Musicians: Linda Thompson (vocals, harmony vocals, chorus),
Jenny Muldaur (harmony vocals), Martha Wainwright (harmony vocals),
Antony Hegarty (harmony vocals), Susan McKeown (harmony vocals,
chorus), Janine Nichols (chorus), Kamila Thompson (harmony vocals,
backing vocals), The Barbershop Quartet Round Midnight featuring
Larry Bobmack (tenor), T.J. Carello (lead), Wayne Grimmer (baritone)
and Jeff Glemboski (bass), Teddy Thompson (acoustic guitar, piano,
backing vocals, harmony vocals), David Mansfield (mandolin, acoustic
guitar, electric guitar), Jeff Hill (electric bass, double bass), George Javori
(drums, dumbek, tambourine, percussion), Bill Dobrow (shakers),
John Kirkpatrick (Anglo concertina, button accordion), John Doyle
(acoustic guitar), John Joe Kelly (bodhran), Rob Burger (Hammond
organ, pump organ), Brad Albetta (double bass), Larry Campbell (fiddle),
James Walbourne (electric guitar), Eliza Carthy (Hohner organetta,
harmony vocals), Martin Carthy (acoustic guitar), The Downtown Silver
Band featuring Steven Bernstein (alto horn, flugelhorn), Frank London
(alto horn, cornet) and Dan Levine (euphonium, tuba), Maxim Mostin
(violins), Antoine Silverman (violin), David Creswell (viola), Anja Wood
(cello), Byron Isaacs (double bass), Rob Moose (nylon string guitar,
violins) and The Scorchia Quartet featuring Gregor Kitzis (violin),
Paul Woodiel (violin), Martha Mooke (viola) and Leah Coloff (cello)
Stay Bright/Versatile Heart/The Way I Love You/Beauty/Katy Cruel/
Nice Cars/Do Your Best For Rock'n'Roll/Day After Tomorrow/

Discographies

Blue & Gold/Give Me A Sad Song/Go Home/Whisky, Bob Copper And Me/Stay Bright

Won't Be Long Now (Topic Records, UK, 2013)
Produced by Edward Haber
Musicians: Linda Thompson (vocals, harmony vocals, chorus), Richard Thompson (acoustic guitar), John Doyle (acoustic guitar), Amy Helm (harmony vocals), Sam Amidon (acoustic guitar, banjo), David Mansfield (Weissenborn guitar, mandolin), Kamila Thompson (vocals, harmony vocals, backing vocals), Muna Thompson Mascolo (harmony vocals), Teddy Thompson (acoustic guitar, harmony vocals, backing vocals), Jack Thompson (electric bass), Zak Hobbs (lead and rhythm guitar, mandolins, acoustic guitar), Gerry Conway (drums), Glenn Patscha (piano, Hammond organ, pump organ), Dave Swarbrick (fiddle), Martin Carthy (acoustic guitar), Garo Yeliln (cello), Eliza Carthy (melodeons, lead and chorus vocals), Susan McKeown (lead and chorus vocals, backing vocals), Jeff Hill (electric bass), George Javori (drums), John Kirkpatrick (button accordion), Rob Burger (Hammond organ), Jason Crigler (acoustic and electric guitar, backing vocals), James Walbourne (electric slide guitar), Jenny Muldaur (backing vocals), Tony Trischka (banjo), Brad Albetta (electric bass), Bill Dobrow (percussion).
Love's For Babies And Fools/Never Put To Sea Boys/If I Were A Bluebird/As Fast As My Feet/Father Son Ballad/Nursery Rhyme Of Innocence And Experience/Mr Tams/Paddy's Lamentation/Never The Bride/Blue Bleezin' Blind Drunk/It Won't Be Long Now

Family (Decca Records, UK, 2014)
Producer: Teddy Thompson
Musicians: Linda Thompson (Vocals), Richard Thompson (Guitar, Goblet Drums, Hurdy Gurdy, Vocals), Teddy Thompson (Guitar, Harmonium, Piano, Bass, Vocals), Kami Thompson (Vocals), Muna Thompson Mascolo (Vocals), James Walbourne (Guitar, Bass, Vocals), Rob Walbourne (Percussion), Zak Hobbs (Guitar, Mandolin, Vocals), Brooke Gengras (Vocals), Paulina Lis (Vocals),
Family/One Life At A Time/Careful/Bonny Boys/Roots So Bitter/At The Feet Of The Emperor/Right/Perhaps We Can Sleep/That's Enough/I Long For Lonely

Notes & Sources

¶

1 Colin Irwin *The Guardian* 24th March 2011
2 Colin Irwin *The Guardian* 24th March 2011
3 Britta Sweers, *Electric Folk*: *The Changing Face Of English Traditional Music*
4 Britta Sweers, *Electric Folk*: *The Changing Face Of English Traditional Music*
5 J.P. Bean, *Singing from the Floor: A History Of British Folk Clubs*
6 BBC, *Folk Britannia*
7 Mark Cooper *The Guardian* 29th December 1988
8 Patrick Humphries, *Richard Thompson: Strange Affair*
9 Alexis Petridis *The Guardian* 31st January 2006
10 J.P. Bean, *Singing From The Floor: A History Of British Folk Clubs*
11 Christy Moore, *One Voice: My Life In Song*
12 Britta Sweers, *Electric Folk*: *The Changing Face Of English Traditional Music*
13 BBC, *Folk Britannia*
14 www.gaudela.net
15 www.gaudela.net
16 http://news.bbc.co.uk/1/hi/entertainment/1347199.stm
17 Derek Schofield, Tim Hart obituary *The Guardian*, 2009
18 J.P. Bean, *Singing From The Floor: A History Of British Folk Clubs*
19 *R2* May/June, 2010
20 Robin Denselow, Tim Hart obituary *The Guardian*, 2009
21 www.mustrad.org.uk
22 *R2* January/February 2008
23 *R2* January/February 2008
24 *R2,* January/February 2008
25 Peter Paphides *The Guardian* 10th February 2011
26 Nick Coleman *The Independent* 2nd September 2007
27 William McIlvanney, *The Papers Of Tony Veitch*

28 http://www.indexmagazine.com/interviews/linda_thompson.shtml
29 *R2* November/December 2013
30 http://www.indexmagazine.com/interviews/linda_thompson.shtml
31 *Ibid*
32 *Ibid*
33 www.womensliberationmusicarchivefiles.wordpress.com
34 http://www.indexmagazine.com/interviews/linda_thompson.shtml
35 Britta Sweers, *Electric Folk*: *The Changing Face Of English Traditional Music* quoting Karl Dallas from a 1966 edition of *Melody Maker*
36 *Ibid*
37 John Harris *The Guardian* 6th May 2005
38 Rob Young, *Electric Eden: Unearthing Britain's Visionary Music*
39 *Rock On* liner notes
40 John Harris *The Guardian* 6th May 2005
41 *R2* May/June 2008
42 http://www.indexmagazine.com/interviews/linda_thompson.shtml
43 Colin Irwin, *Melody Maker* 7th October 1978
44 www.islam.uga.edu
45 www.nimatullahi.org
46 *Ibid*
47 *Ibid*
48 Tim Cummings *The Independent* 12th November 2013
49 *Q* magazine December 1998
50 *Q* magazine December 1998
51 Rob Young *Electric Eden*
52 http://www.rollingstone.com/music/lists/100-best-albums-of-the-eighties-20110418/richard-and-linda-thompson-shoot-out-the-lights-20110315
53 *Ibid*
54 *Ibid*
55 *Ibid*
56 http://www.indexmagazine.com/interviews/linda_thompson.shtml
57 Charles Bermant *The Globe And Mail* 6th April 1985
58 http://mainlynorfolk.info/steeleye.span/records/spanningtheyears.html#notes
59 www.britannica.com
60 *Ibid*

61 http://mainlynorfolk.info/steeleye.span/records/spanningtheyears.html

62 *Ibid*

63 *Sing Out!* 1994

64 Rob Young, *Electric Eden*

65 *The Independent* 22nd February 1995

66 www.thepuredrop.com.au

67 John Tobler *Silly Sisters* album liner notes

68 J.P. Bean, *Singing From The Floor*

69 *Folk Roots* 1988 reproduced at http://mainlynorfolk.info/steeleye.span/articles/maddy88/

70 Fred Dellar, *NME* 2nd October 1976

71 *Airs And Graces* liner notes

72 http://mainlynorfolk.info/steeleye.span/records/spanningtheyears.html#notes

73 *Ibid*

74 *Sing Out!* 1994

75 http://mainlynorfolk.info/steeleye.span/records/spanningtheyears.html#notes

76 Britta Sweers, *Electric Folk: The Changing Face Of English Traditional Music*

77 Peter Paphides *The Guardian* 10th February 2011

78 http://www.bbc.co.uk/music/reviews/3h9x

79 Peter Paphides, *The Guardian* 10th February 2011

80 www.boycottingtrends.blogspot.co.uk

81 www.boycottingtrends.blogspot.co.uk

82 Peter Paphides, *The Guardian* 10th February 2011

83 Tim Cooper, *Evening Standard* 29th July 2003

84 Tim Cooper, *Evening Standard* 29th July 2003

85 http://www.vanderbilthealth.com

86 Patrick Humphries, *Richard Thompson: Strange Affair*

87 *R2* November/December 2013

88 Patrick Humphries, *Richard Thompson: Strange Affair*

89 http://www.ubuprojex.com

90 http://www.indexmagazine.com/interviews/linda_thompson.shtml

91 www.maddyprior.co.uk

92 www.rosekemp.info

93 www.carnivalband.com

94 www.carnivalband.com

95 *Folk Roots* 1988 reproduced at http://mainlynorfolk.info/steeleye.
span/articles/maddy88/

96 www.andy-cutting.co.uk

97 www.andy-cutting.co.uk

98 www.andy-cutting.co.uk

99 Robin Denselow, *The Guardian* 15th September 2011

100 http://www.bbc.co.uk/news/entertainment-arts-16954049

101 http://www.topicrecords.co.uk/?s=Linda+Thompson

102 Robin Denselow http://www.theguardian.com/music/2013/oct/10/
linda-thomson-wont-be-long-review

103 Jim Wirth http://www.uncut.co.uk/linda-thompson-wont-be-long-
now-review

104 Martin Chilton 21st November 2014 http://www.telegraph.co.uk/
culture/music/worldfolkandjazz/11245124/Thompson-Family-
Family-album-review.html

105 Michael Hann 13th November 2014 http://www.theguardian.
com/music/2014/nov/13/thompson-family-review-richard-linda-
thompson

106 http://www.salon.com/2013/10/27/linda_thompson_good_art_cant_
be_depressing/

107 *Heydays* liner notes

108 *Heydays* liner notes

109 *Hark! The Village Wait* liner notes

110 *Hark! The Village Wait* liner notes

111 *Hark! The Village Wait* liner notes

112 *Woman In The Wings* liner notes

113 *Seven For Old England* liner notes

114 *A Tapestry Of Carols* liner notes

115 *Ashore* liner notes

Three books which proved particularly indispensable in my research were
J.P. Bean's *Singing From The Floor: A History Of British Folk Clubs* (Faber &
Faber), Britta Sweers' *Electric Folk: The Changing Face of Traditional English
Music* (Oxford University Press) and *Electric Eden: Unearthing Britain's
Visionary Music* (Faber & Faber) by Rob Young. Another vital resource

was the excellent website, www.mainlynorfolk.info, which began in 1996 as a fans' site for Steeleye Span and Sandy Denny, and has since evolved into a comprehensive overview of recorded traditional and contemporary English folk music.

Selective Index Of Names

Index does not include the introduction and discography

❡

Selective Index Of Names

About The Author

❡

David Burke is an Irish writer from Mullingar exiled in Wolverhampton. A television subtitler by day and contributor to *R2* and *Vintage Rock* magazines by moonlight, he has authored three books, *Crisis In The Community: The African Caribbean Experience Of Mental Health*, *Heart Of Darkness: Bruce Springsteen's Nebraska* and *A Sense Of Wonder: Van Morrison's Ireland*.

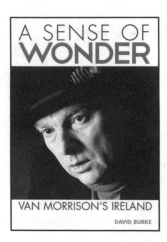

Praise for A Sense of Wonder: Van Morrison's Ireland

"Where Burke especially succeeds is in following a path through both Van's personal history and songs, expanding on the characters and incidents with the relaxed, welcoming prose the reader might expect from a Roddy Doyle novel." *Record Collector*

"David Burke manages to avoid the dreaded Pseud's Corner approach to a musician as inscrutable as he is inspired by showing the subject so much love - and enough genuine insight - to make some passages sing almost as well as their subject." www.mudkiss.com

A Sense of Wonder is a stimulating, highly readable book that anyone interested in Van Morrison will savour." www.culturenorthernireland.org

ISBN: 9781908279484

Jawbone Press 2013

ALSO AVAILABLE FROM SOUNDCHECK BOOKS

Wayward Daughter: An Official Biography Of Eliza Carthy

By Sophie Parkes

ISBN: 9780956642073

"Crucially, the book manages to do justice to the woman herself: earthy, forthright and eminently entertaining." *fRoots*

"Is 'Wayward Daughter' a good biography? Indeed it is. Is it recommended reading? Without a doubt. What are you waiting for? Buy it now." Tim Carroll, *Folkwords*